EMERGING
MARKETER

ENGAGING TODAY'S USERS,
PURSUING TOMORROW'S MEDIA

SHAWN RORICK

Acknowledgement

01000110 01101111 01110010 00100000 01010011 01110100
01100101 01110000 01101000 01100001 01101110 01101001
01100101 00101100 00100000 01110111 01101000 01101111
00100000 01101110 01100101 01110110 01100101 01110010
00100000 01100110 01100001 01101001 01101100 01110011
00100000 01110100 01101111 00100000 01110010 01100101
01101101 01101001 01101110 01100100 00100000 01101101
01100101 00100000 00100010 01111001 01101111 01110101
00100000 01100011 01100001 01101110 00100000 01100100
01101111 00100000 01101001 01110100 00100010 00101110

PREFACE

To simply say "the world is changing" has become an understatement. Not only is the world changing, but the changes are happening with more frequency and intensity. Most of us in the digital marketing community realize *change* to be an ongoing circumstance we must embrace to remain successful in our own industries. The speed of information (a contributor to change) is growing exponentially at an alarming rate, which means the demand for us to perform using leading-edge technologies is increasing.

Seeking the answer to next-generation advertising and marketing tactics is easy. The tough part is determining if those new methods of marketing are applicable. Or better yet, when are they worthy of our investment? Marketers face major dilemmas today within this realm. Management demands that we employ the latest-greatest, yet we know that many of these so-called emerging platforms may be a waste of time ... for now.

Gone are the days of Internet advertising exclusivity. Today we are looking at mediums merging with offline media. Mobile (SMS) marketing, social media, widgets, in-game placements, rich media and other formats are becoming an impending factor we have to weigh in with our budgets and time resources. Not everything is going to turn out to be a "home run" when it comes to

ROI success. But the plain fact is that we won't know if we don't try.

In 2005 I was asked to write a book about Internet marketing and the many different aspects of consumer engagement using this fairly new media. I locked myself in a hotel room for five days and pounded out everything I could think of, from search marketing to display advertising and ROI metric tracking using current ad-serving technologies. After finishing over half of the book, I stopped and read what I had written. I realized I had only mapped out what I felt would be relevant to the masses for the next couple of years. Little did I know that offline, traditional marketers would be compelled to embrace the world of digital media for years to come as new exchanges in communication continue to emerge.

The forms of online advertising we have been using are becoming obsolete for a variety of reasons. Whether it is the long tail of media applications, technologies assisting users in ad blocking, or the fact that consumers are using search in different ways; the old tactics are becoming more and more difficult to garner the returns we have been used to reporting and proudly presenting to our employers.

Looking at the variety of media today and the multiple opportunities we have before us to engage the consumer is staggering. One cannot possibly set out to use *every* single method available. The astute marketer knows his business, knows the consumer profiles for his industry, and can get a good sense of whether or not these tactics and placements are a viable play for him.

But then again *everyone* has a cell phone, *everyone* plays video games, almost *everyone* and their mother has a blog, almost *everyone's* cell phone is Bluetooth-equipped, and *everyone* uses search as a resource to manage their daily life. So the past strategy of attaching your particular business demographic to particular media use is out the window. Humanity has created for itself a buffet of technology-driven resources to determine when, where and how they will consume media.

If you've historically been an "offline" marketer, focusing on print, radio, TV, etc., you are reaching a time where "interactive" marketing is playing a role in the day-to-day management of your business. Likewise, if you've been an "online" marketer in the past, then you're starting to see that your users, acquisitions, conversions and page view metrics aren't the only way to measure your audience in the emerging media space.

The days of "offline" and "online" specialty categorization are over; we are all "interactive" marketers in the 21st century - two separate disciplines being brought together after a decade of dissonance from one another. The only way we are going to evolve and become *better* in our own careers is to learn from each other and tap one another's resources for more knowledge. Social Media = PR. Telemarketing = Mobile Marketing. In-game Advertising = Outdoor Advertising.

Emerging Marketer has been written to open eyes on the new and the realistic expectations we should have on using emerging marketing technologies. Right now, they may seem like a small sliver of our budgets. However, it is my firm belief (using other cultures' adaptations, spending growth and online consumer behavior as a basis) that these new forms will take on more and more responsibility to deliver our bottom line.

In 2005 I realized that my goal shouldn't be to focus on what is today and how to get there. It should be to present what is emerging today and *when* to get there. *Emerging Marketer* won't expand your knowledge on what you are already doing. The intention is to open your mind to where you should be headed and where your thoughts should be to propel you to success over the next 10+ years.

I don't expect everyone to agree with all points outlined in this book. There are great professionals with names already out there who have brilliant minds. But there's one thing we can all agree on; the more we discuss, debate, test, trial, study, research and engage – the faster we will move forward as a society with the right footsteps toward our shifting audience.

Over the years I've had tremendous support from friends, family and co-workers to educate audiences with experiential knowledge and foresight on marketing, technology and new media. Before diving into discussion, I'd like to thank everyone for their encouragement and positive influence to get me out from "behind the curtain." Surrounding yourself with good people is something that should never be overlooked as you continue down your own personal career path.

Enjoy!

Chapter I
Where to Start

The first chapter of any book is critical, as readers start here to see how a literary work was written, what it's going to teach, how the writing style flows, etc. *Emerging Marketer* exposes all the latest-greatest in marketing and media technology available to us today. However, there is a certain segment of readers that should be addressed so *everyone* learns what they need to by reading the forthcoming chapters and pages.

If you are a seasoned Internet or interactive marketer, please feel free to skip forward. But you just might want to stick around for a bit, as this part of the book discusses the different views of individuals based on their involvement in this space. Plus maybe, just maybe, you'll get a little more insight into how to approach emerging media when learning about it for the first time.

"Newbies" to interactive marketing as well as formerly *traditional offline* marketers often wonder where and how to jump in this game. After all, it seems there are a ton of Internet marketers out there who have been around the block and have obviously made their mark. You'll soon find out that you are not alone *and* the so-called veterans have to start on a level playing field in some cases within this day and age, just as you are.

For the First-timer

New advances in technology that yield marketing opportunities can be pretty overwhelming. There are thousands of blogs, email newsletters, media feeds and news resources out there that point to the different media outlets, best practices and everything else you supposedly *should be doing*. If you wrap your arms around all the information published each day, the primary practical areas discussed and applicable to today's interactive marketer are the following:

Search Marketing	Social Media
Mobile Marketing	Virtual World
In-game Advertising	Video Placement
Viral Campaigns	Rich Media
Gadgets/Widgets	Desktop Applications
Web Metrics/Tracking	Interactive TV

Each individual area has its own list of specific characteristics, associated executions and applicable audiences. After reading this book it is vitally important that you continue to follow the channels you feel are most applicable to your business. Emerging media is always changing and not a one-time "stop and shop" for consumers. But if you venture into one area and become a leader for your industry using that channel, it means this book has served its purpose and set you down a path that will be developing for years to come.

If you've decided it's time to become more 21st century in the way you market and advertise products and services, congratulations. You've just decided to stick around in the workforce a little longer. It was only a few years ago that I attended a conference where the keynote clearly stated, "If you don't understand Internet marketing within the next five years, you'll be looking for a job." Lo and behold, here we are just a few years later and I see Internet marketing not only as education on the rise but as a concrete part of media plan foundations everywhere.

But as we move from this general knowledge base and understanding around Internet marketing, how is it going to evolve? And how have the other media channels such as television and radio evolved at the same time? Where is the best place to learn and test out these new forms of media for your business?

These are questions I hope to have answered within these pages. The good news is that most of these areas are still new enough that everyone is asking the same questions. Yes, even you seasoned online professionals who are still reading!

Before diving into any area of emerging media, I've always found it best to ask myself four elementary questions:

1) Is this where my consumer is?
2) Is the cost of entry prohibitive at this time?
3) Are my competitors using this space? *With success?*
4) Do case studies exhibit the returns I'm looking for?

These may seem like "duh" questions, but you'd be surprised how many marketing professionals get caught up in the *hype*. Everyone wants to tout the next big thing, but the bottom line is that it makes sense for *your* business.

Take, for example, in-game advertising. Based on the overall demo- and psychographic makeup of this audience, certain brands have found it to be very rewarding in terms of the lift they get for overall purchase intent. But other companies looking for a direct revenue impact simply aren't going to find it here. Why? Because technology is still a tad bit behind the availability for the masses to interact, research and purchase within this media.

Every activity you engage will depend on your objectives. In many cases, you will need to clearly establish *branding* versus *direct response/revenue* goals before embarking on a lot of these outlets. If the goal is audience, then resulting sales shouldn't be the deciding metric of success. It's always best to establish these criteria *before* you launch your campaign. Too many times I've seen folks try to jump in and poke holes at a successful branding excursion when conversions and sales shouldn't have been the objective in the first place.

Also know that before jumping into anything you should be sure to test, observe, assess and test again. Test as much as you need to in order to convince yourself. Emerging media is moving fast but not so fast that you need to invest a lot of upfront money to get your feet wet. Remember that everyone playing in these channels is new to them and doing the same thing ... evaluating.

Evaluation Can Be a Daunting Task

Say you've tried mobile media and didn't get the results you are looking for. What does that mean? Does it mean you abandon it and turn toward something else? Did you spend enough money to begin with? Did you include a call to action? Was it targeted appropriately?

With more monthly text messages than phone calls, it's going to be tough to walk away. Marketers are plagued with "could-have", "should-have", "would-have" scenarios after the fact, which can drive some of us mad. The frustration behind knowing a media channel will work and then finding out it was a waste of time and money can be daunting.

A close friend of mine who is the executive advertising vice president for a major resort in Las Vegas has certainly undergone the throes of mobile media. Testing, testing and more testing is what he's accomplished. But each time he dabbles, there is a new revelation. He went as far as to speak at an event I hosted where several mobile marketing service providers were present. His opening comments along with the rest of his speech went into all the failures they have had. Needless to say, at the end he blatantly stated that in his heart he knows this is the way of the future.

Since that time, nothing has stopped them from more testing. Today, they are the most recognized cutting-edge resort, setting the pace for everyone else in mobile media strategy.

My advice to everyone looking to test is to make sure you have enough fuel to endure repetitive trials. The worst thing I can think of is to use time and resources toward emerging media that are thrown out if it doesn't work the first time around. There are no written rules in play; you have to make them for yourself. If you can't afford it, don't bother. Most of the time emerging media eventually becomes cheaper as it is acclimated into the practices of most marketers.

Emerging media isn't something you simply choose to try once with a service provider or on your own. It's a realm where your participation and *consistent* involvement is required to reap the rewards you seek. While I'm not a big advocate of spending a lot of money on new tactics or channels in my own workplace, I definitely know that my involvement in my industry with new media helps shape the world to come.

Marketers hold the key when determining the longevity of media. One could argue that the consumers of media are the owners of the space, meaning that the adoption of specific channels ultimately decides if a particular medium lives a long life. I'd argue that if there's no money behind advertising to support the next-gen technology, it won't be around long. Just look at all the Web sites that have failed because they didn't monetize their audience.

It is up to all of us to help shape the future of emerging media. Whether you test it, reject it or accept it, you are assisting in the movement of mountains. I always appreciate reading about a competitor's case study in media testing because it gives me a better understanding of how to apply it to my business or if I should even bother!

Perspectives of the Players

Your perceptions of emerging media will also vary based on your background. Marketing is such a general area where there are many different "fields" in which one could choose to specialize. With regard to any high-tech channel I encounter, including Internet media, there are four different professional backgrounds that observe things just a little differently from everyone else.

It's important to realize this, as a lot of your own research within the emerging media space will yield varying commentary from many different people. Understanding their backgrounds will help you understand not just how they view things but *why* they see things in a certain light. Some will be helpful, others may be cynical, but each of them will eventually be affected by media that is adopted by the masses.

The Marketers –

Marketers, in general, have an optimistic view toward new opportunities to gain more ground in the eyes of their consumers (and employers). As mentioned, marketing is a general area. So you can expect, when talking to the average marketer, to get an *overview* perspective. Emerging media is often summarized in a statement that incorporates their knowledge of common-denominators and research/case studies they've read.

Marketers are learning that today's emerging media is quickly becoming tomorrow's new media. They are competitive and reluctant to share information with competitors in their field. They are also eager to learn from everyone they talk to in order to gain an advantage.

When it comes to emerging media, general marketers are ready to jump in, provided there have been plenty of tests, evaluations and case studies. One thing's for sure - you'll never get a convoluted position. Seasoned marketers, especially, are more than ready to take a pro- or anti-position with media.

The *Internet* Marketers –

Within this group you will find the early adopters. They were the ones that took a leap of faith (whether they knew it or not) to jump into the online world and forgo their potential success in offline media. These individuals always have an optimistic view toward new technologies in advertising. After all, they've already witnessed the power of their own internet channels.

You'll also find a bit of confusion with these professionals as they sift through the different components of emerging channels. For instance, is social media a PR application or an Internet marketing application? If SMS revolves around cellular devices, does it belong to the Internet marketers? They are constantly asking these questions as they decide how they are going to enter and engage these channels.

Regardless of their disposition, Internet marketers are used to being trendsetters, so they are more than prepared and experienced to test and assess. More than likely, they have made their employers (or themselves, if self-employed) very happy when it comes to ROI. Now that Internet marketing as we know it has matured, they are all looking for another area in which to specialize.

The Developers –

Don't bother talking in terms of potential revenue with this group. Developers look at things in a completely different way. They are purists at heart and develop media around what they think is best for the users. You'll find both pessimists and optimists, depending on how ambitious they are about adding to their own skill set to play in emerging media. To them, media is about content and its delivery.

It used to frustrate me to no end how the developers I've known seemed to be so stubborn about the implications of new media and the potential revenue. Over the years, I've come to understand that new tactics for advertising and marketing wouldn't exist if it wasn't for these individuals. They constantly feel the need to stand behind the whole church-vs.-state concept as they develop around what the users will appreciate, not necessarily thinking about the bottom line.

Looking past this positioning, you'll find a wealth of information. They can explain estimated costs, some audience metrics as well as provide an insight into what they think would be the best message or content to use to attract your customers. Just don't tell them you are looking to maximize conversions from your newly found audience.

The Media Sales Professionals –

Perspectives retained by sales people always revolve around the audience size. They inherently know that with the audience come advertisers and their budgets. Thus, they depend on their sales to generate an income for themselves. Just as all media sales professionals do.

It always amazes me when my staff or others I know steer away from the account executive looking to close an advertising agreement with them. Certainly you have those who are too pushy and sometimes unprofessional in their approach. But the majorities I have encountered have maintained their composure and are pleasant to deal with. Plus, they can be the most informative.

Always remember, this segment of the marketing population is on the front lines. Chances are they met with your competition recently to sell them the same product. They know the ins and outs of a particular media and can provide extremely valuable insight into what's happening in your industry. Sure, they are looking for a sale with you. But turning the tables around and quizzically discussing the overall marketplace for new media can yield some information you may be missing.

Your Competition

Those in your industry competing for the same eyeballs and conversions aren't necessarily your enemy. Personally, I don't feel that emerging media should be kept under wraps, never to be discussed with your competition. We all have our own trade secrets within our practices, and I'm not suggesting we drill so deep that we give away sensitive components. But what you are doing within the emerging media space shouldn't necessarily be coveted.

Some of you are reading this and thinking, "I would never, EVER reveal what I am doing to a competitor." But before taking that stance, keep in mind how fast our media world is moving. Say, for instance, you are trialing a new form of rich media on the Web. If your competition isn't doing the same thing at this point in time, it will probably take them months, perhaps even a year to get to the point where you are now. By that time, you're that much further "ahead" of them in your knowledge base and understanding; probably moving on to something new.

The trick is to think a few steps *ahead* in your competitive strategy. If you aren't able to match them today, what should you be doing to pace with them tomorrow? Take the example of search engines. Google and Yahoo have been paving the way for years and triumph with mass audience and reach. If you go down the rungs on the ladder, you'll find the third tier search engines such as Cuil.com and BlinkX.com suggesting some very innovative tools that look to provide technology *above and beyond* their much larger counterparts.

Competitive Activity

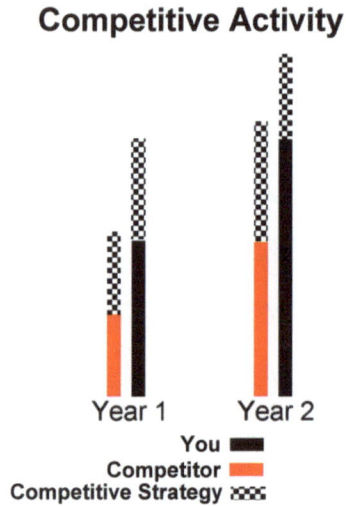

Year 1   Year 2

You ▬
Competitor ▬
Competitive Strategy ▩

Discussing your excursions with your competition can be healthy in your efforts to take the next best step you can toward emerging media. Sharing ideas and experiences only adds more insider knowledge to your work and can give you an advantage over everyone else. Your competitor at a personal level is just like you, thirsty for information. In most experiences, the professional marketer can offer just enough tidbits of information in order to garner a reciprocated conversation with their counterparts.

Sometimes, letting someone else take the first step and gathering subsequent learnings can really propel your efforts into a successful future. Remember, to be *first* is not always *best*.

Chapter II
Where We've Been

It was a Tuesday morning in 1997, with unusual rain for Las Vegas. I was working as a Marketing Director for a Resident Agent - a company that created corporations in the state of Nevada so outside companies could take advantage of privacy, asset protection and tax benefits. It wasn't the most exciting job in the world, but it was where I made the conscious career decision to embark on the Internet marketing journey.

The call came late that morning from the company's founder and CEO. I walked into his office, and he plainly stated that our company needed a Web site for marketing and ecommerce. I had never heard of a Web site at the time that would be able to provide the functionality necessary to be as intrinsic in education and corporate filings as our consultants were via phone. But I was up to the challenge, so I started the research.

This was during a time when Web sites were just on the fringe of development explosion, with many users still on a dialup connection. I had no idea where to begin, so I started with our own Internet service provider. They said they didn't have any webmasters on staff, as they only hosted sites and provided connectivity services. I continued to call agencies, IT companies and anyone I could think of who might be able to throw something together for us. Apparently Vegas was a dead end for a quest of this nature.

So I decided to reach out to the unyielding corporate monstrosity at the time – Microsoft®. With all the press circulating about them, I felt as though I was about to have a conversation with the devil himself. After a few pass-arounds, I reached one of their consumer specialists, who recommended I buy their Web development product, FrontPage 97. A few days later it reached my desk, and I began to create my first Web site.

It didn't take long to later realize the software itself was a cursed disaster and one of the worst Web editors out there, but the technical manual about CGI scripting and HTML development handled most of my road blocks. After a few weeks, my company had what may have been the most unattractive excuse for a Web site - complete with a news ticker. But it worked. It provided information, used a mile-long form to incorporate people, and even allowed opt-ins for email newsletters.

Dogpile, WebCrawler, InfoSpace and Yahoo were some of the biggest search engines on the Web in that day. The site was indexed, and I was happy when I saw it listed first under "Nevada incorporation services" search terms. Needless to say, I didn't realize I had created the first online incorporation form on the Web at that time. After a few weeks of being indexed and promoted through banner-sharing programs, the sales started rolling in. Creating and marketing a platform that brought in more than $30,000 just in overnight sales from foreign countries lit a fire within me that has yet to be extinguished ... even if it wasn't "my" money. After a few months of this my employer was offering a decent incentive to stay and continue the management of their marketing initiatives, but I already had my sights set on venturing more into the online world of development and marketing.

Although none of my higher education taught me this technology, I was determined to educate myself in programming languages and become a specialist in the newborn world of online advertising. Little did I know at the time, thousands of other marketers were doing the same. We all realized that the Web would play an important role in the wide world of media. This was the year of my personal career decision. It was also a year of "The Great Divide."

The Great Divide

Traditional offline and online marketers have been at odds since the mid '90s. Once Internet marketing became a strong contender for eyeballs and consumers, many would-be traditional marketers turned on their tech instincts and ventured into this new realm with hopes and anticipation of setting their skill sets above the rest. Little did we all know what an uphill battle this was going to be.

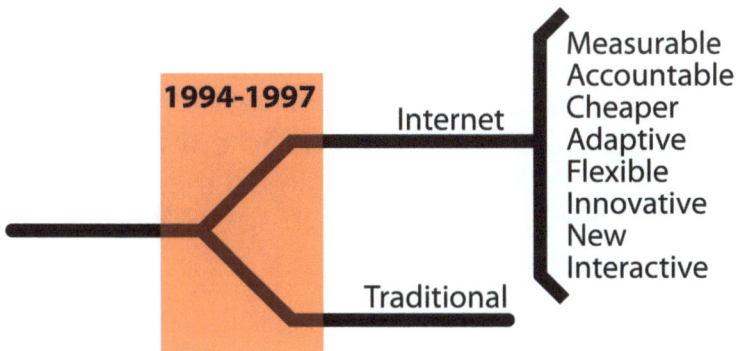

1994-1997

Internet

Measurable
Accountable
Cheaper
Adaptive
Flexible
Innovative
New
Interactive

Traditional

The feuding really started once advertisers were willing to pay top dollar for online advertising. Offline advertising agencies argued that media such as television, direct mail and radio had always been the best resource for branding and revenue. Many of them claimed that the Internet was just a fad that offered unique communication for company messaging. By the turn of the millennium, everyone realized this wasn't the case. Online was here to stay and only getting stronger with progression in reporting and development platforms.

After a few years of consulting and self-education, I found myself working for an online media publisher. The position required that I use both traditional and online marketing disciplines to drive users to our Web site for news, culture, community and tools to manage their daily lives. Our company's success revolved around advertising sales which, at the time (2000-2002), I found was difficult to achieve. But, it also gave me a first-hand glimpse at the traditional media players thumbing their noses at the online space.

With each passing month new case studies emerged, advertising contracts were acquired, and our clients were experiencing more revenue. The shift of advertising dollars from traditional media to the online world had started, and I couldn't have been happier. Online advertising and marketing professionals claimed cheaper market penetration and frequency, more efficient targeting and best of all - actual metrics that traced conversions. And just when offline marketers proclaimed their belief that television was the best media, high-speed connectivity hit its flashpoint ... hello online video.

The next few years brought me to a large hotel and casino group in town, working within an all-too-familiar corporate structure, arguing my points with the offline advertising team, and begging executives to venture more into the space and really open the floodgates on their budgets reserved for traditional media. Online advertising placements and related metric tracking were teeming with opportunities that would trace revenue to the source of placement.

By this time, traditional marketer attitudes had changed just enough to where they felt they should integrate their offline and online initiatives. I remember feeling as though Internet marketers had lost and the traditional side had triumphed while I witnessed agencies begin to buy Internet placements just as they had purchased their radio, television and print advertising in the past. Ad units were purchased at a premium cost-per-thousand (CPM) rate, with ads that targeted Web sites based solely on demographics. Companies everywhere sat back to see what would happen.

As dismal reports of revenue results trickled in, it didn't take long to realize that the Internet didn't respond the same as the offline media that marketers and advertising professionals had been used to. It was dynamic, uncensored and very matter-of-fact when it came to driving consumer conversions. Internet marketing specialists enjoyed a re-emergence of client dedication as advertising budgets were once again shoved in their direction to place advertising based on behavior, context and geo-targeting principles. The expense was low, the revenue was high, and the offline marketers coveted the activity from distant corners.

A Decade of Progression

All of this occurred over the course of 10 years. Whether other cities were ahead of or behind Las Vegas, I speak with marketing folks from all backgrounds who feel the same way. Whether they were on the traditional media side or the Internet marketing side of the fence, everyone seems to be in agreement that this was a 10-year span.

I feel it's important to note that the single factor determining the pace of our online affinity in marketing had to do with the consumer. I make it a point to continually emphasize that the consumer is one of the primary drivers of all emerging media and technology. Whether it is SMS/mobile marketing, social media or in-game advertising, the masses dictate the effectiveness of these channels. It wasn't until 2001 and 2003 that the world saw the fastest growth of consumers jumping online. After which, it wasn't until 2006 when we saw more than 80 percent of households with a high-speed connection. It should, therefore, be no surprise that the largest annual increases in online purchases have only occurred in recent years.

The speed of information has also aided us in the past with the Web's development. As information moves more quickly, we can react faster, with appropriate evaluation and adjustment. If you were to take all the information in the world today, the quantity would double every three years. If you include a half-life value into the equation, you'll see that the speed of information and amount of time it takes to double the world's information correspond exponentially.

The sheer volume of these data is immense. If we were to shove it all into digital memory, it would need to be measured in exabytes (a "1" with 18 "zeros" behind it). Comparatively speaking, if you were to record every word uttered by human lips, it would take up five exabytes of storage.

The rate of our technological evolution comes down to a lot of information moving very fast. It took 10 years for the Internet to really take shape and be understood by all parties. Beyond that decade of development we sit here today and see a new dawn of acclimation. The merging of media has become more apparent as communication, audio, video and interactive technologies have also progressed.

While everyone had their eyes on the Internet as if it were the golden chalice, other media evolutions have snuck up on us. The cell phone is now used to browse the Web, instant message your peers and help us navigate unknown streets. Television now allows us to ignore the programming schedule and watch whatever what we want whenever we want to - commercial free if you keep your thumb on the fast-forward button. Radio reaches audiences well beyond the broadcast boundaries of the towers. Outdoor advertising rotates images and communicates via Bluetooth. Classifieds are free and reach everyone. Our desktop computers readily gather information we are interested in without our input.

Bottom line: It's a great time to be in the advertising and marketing profession.

Compare a few current formats considered to be "emerging media" and their corresponding traditional media attributes. You'll see the similarities in audience measurement and why this allows both offline and online marketers a deeper comprehension of both forms of messaging.

Traditional	Emerging
Telemarketing	Mobile Marketing
Outdoor Advertising	In-game Advertising
Public Relations	Social Media
Logoed Apparel	Widgets and Gadgets

Both online and offline marketers have the opportunity these days to understand the two worlds and address the new media popping up everywhere. It provides an opportunity for the two once-separate specialties to work together and understand each other's disciplines. Each and every marketer experiences a form of technologically driven interactive channels in one way or another on a daily basis. Therefore …

The proper name "Internet marketing" goes away.

Categorization of "traditional" marketers isn't applicable.

We are all now considered "*Interactive Marketers*."

The First Signs of Real "Change"

Fortunately for those who love to adopt new technologies into their advertising plans, the wait is over. Because the speed of information and massive data transfer has become so great, you will all be able to quickly experience the highs of media adaptation. Unfortunately for those who like successful media tactics to stay the same, you've only just begun to feel uncomfortable.

Emerging media beckons us to continuously test, trial and execute, or else we fail. The 10-year adoption of Internet by the masses took eons compared to what we will witness in future generations of media. The evolution of communication is why we will see SMS marketing explode. The availability of high-speed via WiFi™ is why we will witness interactive video match the popularity of television. The fragmentation of device interfaces is why we'll watch widgets and gadgets flood the marketplace. The increased need to be more social by users is why we'll find ourselves in virtual worlds.

In 2004 user-generated content (UGC) was all we could use to explain the interactive results of allowing two-way communications between consumers and companies. Message boards and chat rooms had become a dime-a-dozen and marketers did what they could to assess this as a potential revenue outlet. After a few years, UGC evolved into a component of what is now known as "social media." For many, this is the first time of real "change" we have seen in online user behavior. Perhaps it is the fact that social media is the first activity to really lend itself beyond the boundary of our mouse clicks. As the Web began to feed content into our cell phones, consumers also found their Web communications on their mobile screens.

A friend of mine recently told me that he was interviewing someone as a potential candidate for temporary summer work he had available at his firm. The "interviewee" was on a school break and had come with a glowing commentary by the person that referred him. My friend left a message and asked for the youth to give him a call if he was interested in working for him. Instead of a call, my friend received a text message that said, "Do you want to interview me over the phone or via text?"

We are definitely at the threshold of real change. The new generation will never understand what "rewind" means with this digital age of on-demand TV. They won't understand what it means to have a cassette ruined from melting in your car. I look at my 4 year old today and realize that her future kids, my "grand kids," won't ever use the acronym "CD" to describe something they are listening to.

The most recent, widespread, real-world example of how quickly our communication is changing today was exemplified in the race for 2009 presidential office between John McCain and Barack Obama. ALL political views aside, these two former contenders exhibited big differences in their approaches and the execution of their campaigns to the public. These differences ended up playing a huge role in who would be the next leader of the free world.

McCain's party had many years of experience behind them in the composition of political campaigns. They knew the primary mass media to use in order to reach the right people with the right demographics with the right message. Many of his tactics tapped the same tried-and-true media channels that had been successfully used before. His online presence implemented some blogs and video, but overall they believed in the offline world to carry him to victory.

President Obama's campaign was just as simple, with one exception - his application of emerging media. Everyone above the age of 18 was a vote and an acquisition for support. The candidate with the most acquisitions at the end of the campaign would win. Someone in his party knew there were more ways to hit large audiences than traditional Web site, television, radio, print and outdoor. More importantly, some of the alternative media encompassed the younger demographics frequently missed in the past.

Compare the two candidates and their use of emerging media:

John McCain	Barack Obama
Video Sharing	Video Sharing
Blogs/Social Media	Blogs/Social Media
Mobile (SMS)	Mobile (SMS)
	In-game Advertising
	Viral Campaigns

As marketers, we are always evaluating and attempting to set expectations when it comes to the return on new promotions, advertising tactics or our use of new media. For a minute, take the traditional "bottom line" out of the equation and say the goal is to garner as many people submitting their contact information as possible - such as an email address. Your media channels would change, and you would probably engage channels you wouldn't normally try if you had to show revenue.

This was the approach Obama's team took as they collected votes. No one in history had used in-game advertising as a tactic for presidential election. Viral campaigns were never compelling enough to forward, yet millions of users received the "Be sure to vote" video pushed by the MoveOn.org Political Action Committee. Nor had anyone tapped the penetration and frequency that mobile (SMS) can provide. Obama sent a text message to more than 2.9 million recipients informing everyone who his running mate would be, making it the largest mobile campaign in history. Was it a coincidence that around this time the number of text messages outnumbered phone calls?

As we all know, Obama won the election by a fairly decent margin. Reaching the next generation of technology users was a key factor in his success. Older generations of marketers may look at these new techniques as being nothing more than fads. The presidential election of 2008 certainly exhibited everything it could to contradict that notion.

Through my own research, I've found the average age of Fortune 500 boards of directors to be 55+, or part of the earlier half of the "baby boomer" generation (born between 1946 and 1964). Sit back and think about where this generation has stood with technology at various points in their life. They saw the introduction of color television into the general marketplace in 1964. Motorola's DynaTAC cell phone was first introduced in 1983 for general consumption. Home computers were also introduced in the 1980s. By the time Internet was a commonly used term it was 1996, when they were already around 50 years old.

It is human nature to stray away from that which we don't understand. Personally, I'm convinced that this older demographic influencing mainstream companies today is responsible for the pace at which the marketing usage of emerging media has progressed. It's difficult convincing executive management to trial new channels, especially when those channels involve technology they aren't familiar with. Working with "what works" is always the safest route to go in their minds and, from their perspective, they don't *need* to take on risky expenses. Fortunately, new media today is relatively inexpensive to experiment with and fly under the radar.

The baby boomers are at their last stop in the workforce, as retirement or mortality catches up with them. Soon they will drop out of the equation and another piece of our emerging media progression puzzle will be installed.

The Future
You're hopefully reading this book to gain an insider's advantage with regard to emerging media and how to integrate it into your current marketing activity. While you will certainly gain that information, it will only be useful for a few years. The space you've chosen to play in can change at an alarming rate and still impresses me every day I play alongside you. Media has become a living, breathing, responsive and fragmented beast *with a voice*. Whether you are a seasoned marketer with 30 years of experience or a recent college grad with something to prove, you both have specific advantages.

Long-term experience in the advertising world will assist you, because, like me, you've witnessed the changes. You understand how audiences can change in the way they consume their media and the varied effectiveness for different communications initiatives. This makes it easy to watch the trends happen, assisting you in your prediction of when it's time to engage your business within these channels.

Younger entrepreneurs and marketing graduates have the advantage because they are already using emerging media channels to manage their daily life. They have grown up in a world that allows them to dictate where, when and how they digest their media. This critical aspect gives them the much-sought-after understanding of how to put ourselves in the shoes of consumers today.

Mobile Phone Features Used and Mobile Media Activities of Digital Savvy vs. Total US Adult Consumers, August 2006-March 2007 (% of respondents in each group)

	Digital savvy (n=5,672)	Total (n=111,051)
Text messaging	88%	31%
Camera (pictures)	72%	27%
Download ringtones	66%	20%
Picture messaging	51%	11%
Instant messaging	46%	10%
E-mail	59%	8%
Download video games	38%	8%
Push to talk (2 way)	15%	7%
Stream video clips	19%	2%
Other mobile internet	42%	6%

Note: ages 18+
Source Scarborough Research, "Understanding the Digital Savvy Consumer," May 13, 2008

In 2008 Scarborough Research published a document entitled "Understanding the Digital Savvy Consumer." In the presentation, they outlined specific profiles of this audience group. In summary, digital savvy consumers were defined as:

M (56%) / F (44%)
Median Income: $84,000
Single: 36%
Married w/Children: 38%
College Grad+: 36%

The research also went on to say that over half of the digital savvy were under 34 years old. Seventy-seven percent were under 44. eMarketer™ research clearly shows the differences between this group and the population at large in the way they use technology. Take mobile phone usage for instance. There's a much higher propensity to use mobile devices beyond calling. Text messaging, photos, content downloads and video are all heavily used by this younger audience.

As marketers in the digital age, we are all interested in the digital savvy customer. The downside is that the technology moves very quickly and trends today will dramatically change within just a few years. You will find that truly considering yourself an emerging marketer isn't just about executing what's *new*. It's about foreseeing what's *next*.

Chapter III
Where We're Headed

Whether it's a learned trait or something inherent within you, the ability to see into the future and play your strategy cards accordingly is a huge asset. For those just venturing out into the next generation of marketing technology, it can take years of trend-changing and subsequent monitoring to get a knack for observing the flow of audience preferences. For old-timers who've been around the block a few times, the difficulty to predict may be due to what *they* feel is hot, not necessarily what is actually happening.

For instance, when Twitter first arrived on the scene, many experienced marketers rejected it simply because they didn't use it. They felt that out of all the new forms of communication they used, Twitter simply wasn't one of them so the position was that if *they* aren't using it, not many people are. As everyone knows, this couldn't have been farther from the truth as the power of the Twitter audience has been harvested to drive traffic and attention.

Missing out on "the next big thing" early can have consequences later. I once worked with an individual who felt everything needed to return a profit in order for us to engage in it. While this is a perfectly normal stance to take, what happens if the new media grows so rapidly it costs you more to enter the game later on? Then again, investing too much up front with no return will surely turn upper management off to the whole concept, leaving you to watch as opportunity slides by.

The goal is to find a happy medium (no pun intended) between knowing when to observe, dabble and ultimately "jump in". This can be resolved by maneuvering into position *organically* so as not to create a major bump in your budget down the road.

Seeing the Future

Instead of sitting back and waiting for the direction to be given to you, you've chosen to enter a world where your vision of the future is an absolute. There are a number of tools available today with regard to monitoring and measuring. It's the way you cross-reference data that ultimately determines how you should move forward.

Understanding how fast information travels today, which causes our media outlets to change rapidly, is essential in your prediction of the future. This progression combined with the following factors yields a scenario you can visualize and adopt your strategies toward.

1. *Growth of the Audience*
   Statistics are reported on how many people are engaged in a certain activity. Over time, these numbers usually aggregate new media audiences and report this information as well. Back when the Internet made its debut as a marketing tool, those statistics revolved around the number of people using search engines, visiting Web sites and time spent using email. Today, statistics are available for newer media such as multiplayer gaming and iPhone application users. Monitoring these statistics and measuring monthly or annual growth will help you forecast the explosion.

2. *Ad Spending Projections*
    There are a variety of services you should subscribe
    to that report on monthly, quarterly or annual
    advertising spending on specific media and channels.
    eMarketer™ (the resource used to substantiate some
    of the points made in this book) and other services are
    subscriptions that prove to be extremely helpful, as
    they provide insight on spending patterns for others like
    you. Watching the budget allocation grow provides a
    dotted line into the future. Keep a close eye on where
    your fellow marketers are putting their money.

3. *News Feeds*
    With all the alerts, RSS feeds and search preferences
    available, relevant news feeds can easily be
    monitored for new headlines or releases. It's easy
    to notice publishers and audience-aggregating
    companies tout their growth over time. You can also
    use this to take note of new media or modifications
    within existing media, such as interactive metrics,
    finally developed and noted as a "breakthrough" for a
    particular channel.

4. Your Daily Encounters
    What's that new gadget your kid is constantly messing
    with? The guy next to your cube is talking about a
    new GPS integration into his favorite blog tool. How
    did your friend get that last-minute vacation package
    that saved them $800? These are all instances
    that might pose an insight into an up-and-coming
    marketing opportunity for you. Of course the channel
    needs to fit your product. But taking special note
    of your surroundings and the way people are using
    technology to manage their daily lives may just show
    you the next emerging medium. Take note and
    observe.

Now that you've observed, monitored and determined
the space you need to play in, sit back and decide how
much money, time and effort should be placed on this

lucky number. If you've researched something that is truly emerging media, it's almost a guarantee that this medium isn't saturated with competitors. This provides you some time to maneuver yourself into a dominating position.

Rather than allocating budget right away and jumping in, ask yourself how you can adjust your current resources and strategy to move in the right direction. Project your strategy two, three, even five years from now and envision where your company, product or services need to be in the consumer's eye. Take on a phased approach depending on how far ahead you project, and create a checklist of where you should tweak your marketing and advertising over time to accomplish this. Approaching the new media using this tactic can save you lots money in the long run.

Take the following example:

An interactive marketer observes mobile (SMS) marketing as an emerging media. He's monitored the audience usage and noted the acclimation by international markets as well as certain industries spending their marketing dollars on it. All the signs are there, but the cost of entry is prohibitive. The marketer realizes he needs to take this on someday but probably not for another three years. Using his current email and Web marketing initiatives, his plan may look something like this:

Year 1

-   Add a "mobile number" field to his current email subscription form

-   Include a survey for his online users to discover their affinity for communication via mobile

Year 2

-   Continue to build the database

- Outsource a service to test the numbers he's collected and their responsiveness to messaging

- Implement call-to-actions using a "short code" in all offline advertising

Year 3

- Purchase a short code for the company

- Contract a back-end service provider for SMS

- Execute a direct response campaign using the database he's built.

In this example, it is obvious that mobile marketing without a database doesn't make much sense to jump into. Careful preparation and short-term testing to acquire your database of mobile users as well as ensure they have an affinity for hearing more about your product and potential purchases via their cell phone can take time. No need for a short code if you don't have the database to market to. The speed at which you pull these things together depends on different variables. But this clearly demonstrates how foreseeing the future of media should impact how you modify today's marketing activity.

By the time you approach Year 3, you've collected your audience, tested the responsiveness, and eliminated the cost of building a database.

Today's Failures, Tomorrow's Successes

Some channels deemed to be *emerging* simply phase out and die before our very eyes because there isn't much traction with the audience or apparent returns on our marketing-dollar investment. Take heed in discarding what has been largely tested and tentatively proven to *not* work. We are at a time when the speed of information and popularity can exceed the present need for revenue.

I, personally, had never observed this until my encounter with Second Life, a virtual world created in 2003 by a company called Linden Labs. I remember beta testing a few years prior, before the official launch and well before the mass hysteria that dominated marketing conversations in 2006.

Second Life was created to provide graphic representation to users who integrated their communication into a virtual, "visual" space. The virtual world represents unlimited possibilities in terms of what you can create, wear, look like, act like, and how you engaged peers. Individual *residents,* as they are called, can create their own avatars and interact with other residents and objects within this world.

I remember noting that, with all the graphics and interactions happening, users found the virtual world worthless without a high-speed connection. During the beta version and official launch spanning from 2001-2003, this was indeed a cool tool, yet the availability of technology (high-speed) hadn't caught up with the concept. Regardless, the public tool remained available for anyone looking to dabble. A few years later, marketers began to take notice.

Mid-year 2006, Second Life's population of residents (registered users) had reached 500,000. The media took notice and started splashing the tool as emerging media. It seemed like every day I was receiving at least three newsletters talking about Second Life and how it was this *new playground* for marketers. Case studies and company press releases started to pop up everywhere, almost as if it were an online gold rush.

Much to the dismay of almost everyone I've seen enter this space for marketing purposes, it didn't work. For one, it was a world with new rules that most companies simply weren't ready for. It involved two-way communication, virtual terrorists, and a community that wasn't ready to accept advertising. Millions of dollars that were invested were never reciprocated. The marketers were unprepared for the response they received from the audience.

By 2008, Second Life was barely mentioned in the popular news publications. It still continues to grow today, but without much interest from the marketing community. Interactive marketers felt burned and began to venture in other directions. Virtual world community response was new, and they hadn't learned the rules of engagement.

This encounter really opened up the doors for social media. The blogosphere began to take on a more solid shape, as it offered the same playing field for two-way communication but didn't involve the three-dimensional graphical representation Second Life did. Since then, social media has been embraced, experimented with and tested for revenue returns, while Second Life lies in waiting.

Just as connectivity speeds were a prohibitive factor for the audience back in 2001-2003, the new rules of advertising and marketing prohibited successful entry in 2006-2007. As interactive marketers continue to experience social community and social media, they are equipping themselves with the tools and knowledge it will take to formulate another entry into Second Life. We may see five or even 10 years pass before virtual worlds become a common denominator across interactive marketing plans, but it *will* happen.

This is one example of how emerging media may "emerge" too quickly for both consumers and marketers. It also goes to show that sometimes it's best to dabble instead of jumping in head first. The positive side to this is that it (along with other factors) has forced marketers to understand the social side of two-way media communications before we progress into next-level territories.

The Cloud

While there are different areas we can watch evolve over the next few years, there's also an overall pressing change in media that should be explained. This is, of course, the approaching "cloud." Some call it "cloud computing" or "the Internet cloud." Whatever you want to name it, we are heading toward a world without the conventional accessibility rules we are used to.

Cloud Computing will be discussed more in Chapter XV, but in order to set the tone for the rest of this book, we'll overview what it is and why it is important to us as marketers to keep this concept close to our hearts as we head toward a future at an accelerated rate. It reveals a world that breaks all barriers in terms of connectivity, usability and consumer behavior.

The cloud is our future repository of information. It is the collection of massive servers and memory that allows the world's information to be stored and accessed whenever we need it. Connectivity challenges with high speed and accessibility will be in the past when we reach this age of resourcing. Our continuous dependency and reliance on the Internet to provide the information we need to manage our day-to-day lives will grow and enable the cloud to dominate our lifestyle.

With all software, memory requirements and wireless connection capabilities inherent within the cloud, our environment will be modified to where these aspects will no longer be challenges. In common terms, this means no more LAN lines, bulky housings for hard drives under your desk, software titles at Best Buy or even video stores. Users will find themselves with a basic setup including a monitor and keyboard/interface device.

The cloud also intersects the notion of community. User-generated content was a hot topic a few years ago which gradually progressed into what we deem to be "social media." Every connection has the capability to contribute to this vast sea of information, bringing users closer together, but sometimes farther apart as many tend to prefer conversing via their computer rather than in real life. The interconnectivity of our thoughts and views on various topics will continue to grow while each individual garners an audience.

This is the impending future to keep in mind throughout this book. Knowing the general environment that we are headed toward should give you a foundation of understanding to build from as you theorize how each channel will evolve. Ask yourself how our mobile devices will be incorporated in this new age. How are your rich-media ad units placed and managed? What does this mean with regard to your social media campaigns? How will this change search-engine marketing, the number-one ROI generator in online campaigns today? Where does video fit into the future landscape?

Cloud computing is such a diverse topic that an entire chapter has been dedicated to discussion toward the end of this book. Coupled with the speed of information, our future becomes very fast-paced and unyielding when it comes to change and adaptation. Feel free to skip forward and read more about cloud computing and the fast-paced flow of data we are headed for. Having a concrete idea of what our future entails in broad strokes may help you better understand what your approach should be with emerging media today.

The marketing perspective on the cloud revolves around how users adapt to the changing world. Obviously we'll want to be where our customers are, and if this future continuously brings us new media channels, then each one will need to be tested, evaluated and engaged to the extent that it makes sense for our business. We have to imagine ourselves in the future and put on the shoes of our customers. If the Web and general computing are moving toward a pay-per-use climate, then one may start to see how actual software applications may be a progressed form of communication. Drawing a line between this and widgets/gadgets, we can make the association for today and start steering our efforts in that direction.

Recapping from the previous chapter and taking into account what we've discussed about the speed of information and cloud computing, you can easily see the "perfect storm" we are in the middle of right now. The storm is contributed to by major shifts in audience, generations and professional discipline evolvement, combined with speed of transfer, audience acclimation and resources.

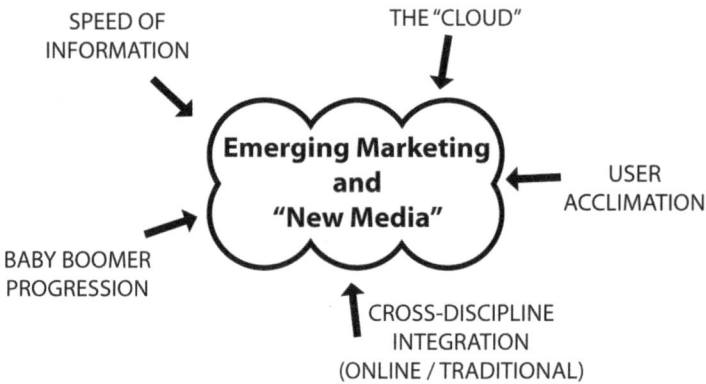

At the end of my speeches around emerging media, I often close with these action items: Discover, Evaluate and Evolve. These terms are the best way to describe what the emerging marketer's perspective should be. I'm often asked for specifics around these words and how they relate to our day-to-day professional marketing strategies and tactics.

Discover
Staying "in the know" and continuously staying abreast of new developments and consumer products must be ingrained in your thinking. Marketers viewing this as "part of their job" will fail. The discovery trait is one which we might as well incorporate into our own DNA in order to survive in the workplace with our knowledge staying in

demand. News feeds, tech publications, conferences, interactive marketing associations, advertising sales representatives and email newsletters are all resources we have to feed us the information we crave.

Discovery isn't an exercise, nor is it an objective. It is a daily action item that we must place as top priority if we are to succeed in emerging media. This should eventually be a natural motive, subconsciously driven. The unfortunate aspect is that you can't play in the emerging media world at will. With the speed of information moving as quickly as it does, closing your eyes for even a few seconds could lead to missing a huge movement or trend that will take time to catch. For example, let's say that instead of specializing in buying media and driving revenue, you wanted to explore your creative side. You've always had a knack for branding and creative development, plus your years of experience in Photoshop or Premier are screaming for some attention. You ultimately decide to go into graphic design for a few years. After a while, you realize you were happier purchasing media and using innovative tactics to drive revenue. Based on the speed of information today, you would be six years behind the knowledge of media progression.

Maintaining the knowledge around growing media topics and next-generation advertising is a commodity in itself. Your value as an employee goes up with experience and knowledge. Discovery should never be viewed as a task but more as a necessity.

Evaluate
While the "Discover" initiative is something that everyone can do, the "Evaluation" is what yields exclusive knowledge to you as a marketer. Evaluation comes from tests and trials you execute when trying out new advertising or marketing ventures. The results are stored as competitive knowledge in our memory banks and used to move forward when making decisions. The importance

of this comes from a separation of what anyone can do (Discover) from what you have done (Evaluate).

When you evaluate a test that you've engaged, you come out with conclusive data suggesting your next steps. It's vital to ensure you've tested using the right control groups and comparisons to conclude you have dissected your trials and come up with the most comprehensive evaluation possible. The evaluation, after all, will be used as a foundation for deciding which way to go next. Keeping this information to yourself maintains your differentiation and allows your next moves to be your own, not on the tails of your competitors.

Case studies are another positive outcome of this action item. Reading case studies from within industries other than your own may allow you to draw conclusions, depending on how well you know your audience. They can save you time and money as long as they correlate with your own customers. Consider any relevant case study part of the "Evaluate" action item.

Evolve
After Evaluate comes Evolve. This is action you are taking with any decision you make after you evaluate your test results or another case study. Whether it is a minor choice, such as incorporating video into your online ad units, or a major move, such as allocating 20 percent of your marketing budget to mobile (SMS) marketing, the step you take is helping your company to "Evolve."

It goes without saying that evolution in the way we advertise will need to happen in order to keep us on top. All steps lead to this, helping you gain the confidence, approvals and support to evolve the way you need to. Evolution in media takes place in each of the principles that underlie marketing. College course "Marketing 101" at every university teaches these principles called

"The 4 Ps of Marketing" where evolution perspectives can be applied.

- Product – Evolution in product characteristics, making them more appealing to the consumer

- Price – Evolution in how pricing models work for your industry as technology becomes cheaper or benefits become more enhanced

- Placement (Distribution) – Evolution of distribution channels into "emerging media," becoming more complex and multi-faceted

- Promotion – Evolution within our own promotional strategies, conforming to emerging media channels and how we embrace new forms of interaction between us and our consumers

Chapter IV
Social Media

Perhaps the biggest topic within the online marketing world today is social media. It's an area that has evolved over the years as we have evolved as users. Technology has made it more and more accessible and allowed audiences everywhere to contribute to the knowledge pool of the net. Primarily engaged via computers or mobile devices, social media has given consumers a voice and, of course, marketers another avenue to reach them.

The mainstream roots of social media online can be traced back to 1996 with the introduction of GeoCities by Yahoo!. Formerly a neighborhood public posting forum, GeoCities allowed users to create their own Web pages for free and was the first fast-growing service that gave individuals a published, public voice. Chat rooms within the rise of AOL in the early '90s were also a form of social media. But GeoCities sealed the deal when online users were able to publish their work and have it read by others rather than a quick posting in a chat. This was the beginning of the

consumers with a "voice" that we've all come to know and love (or perhaps hate).

As the years went by, message boards and public photo postings became more frequent. Harnessing the content of your users made them engaged and interactive with your brand, which became another hot topic. MySpace took over in 2003 and began to push the envelope with community file sharing and friend networking. It wasn't long until 2005 when YouTube emerged and allowed users to share and comment on video.

Blogging (derived from the term "Weblogs") is also a tool that users can employ individually without community consolidating sites such as MySpace. Hundreds of millions of blogs exist by different authors discussing every topic imaginable. Special services such as WordPress have made blogging platforms extremely accessible and ready for users to begin posting as amateurs. The "Blogosphere," as it has become known, attracts millions of users every month to research, write, comment on and observe.

Today, social media is an enormous characteristic of the Web, as we have truly entered the age of interactivity (Web 2.0). Media has been adopted into the realm of two-way communication, which poses an entirely new dimension for marketers to work within. Here is a forecast for advertising spending in this area:.

US Online Social Network Advertising Spending, 2008-2011 (millions and % change)	
2008	$1,175 (32.9%)
2009	$1,140 (-3.0%)
2010	$1,290 (13.2%)
2011	$1,395 (8.2%)

Source: eMarketer, July 2009

This new age of communication also has an entire list of "new rules" for engagement when it comes to promotional advertising. Posting an ad unit within a popular blog or social community has not proven to be the most effective tactic. Injecting our product or service *contextually* has been the key to harnessing the audiences attracted to this media. Word-of-mouth marketing has been around for ages and has reached a critical point in time where results can be witnessed in a fraction of the time it used to take to come to fruition.

Implementation

Marketers appreciate simplicity. Putting together a promotion, working out the logistics, and buying your media placements were the only steps needed building up to the sit-back-and-watch position. As you will find with most emerging media, the days of the "launch it and leave it" attitude are gone. Our involvement with media today needs to be as frequent as necessary to match the engaged consumer time spent within it. Social media is no exception. In order to attain the results you're looking for, it will be necessary to participate and contribute to the interactive public at large.

Social media endeavors will need to be part of daily operations. Companies who have entered this arena with a message and left have not only missed the opportunity, but have actually lost respect with the audience. Users are privy to marketing and promotional activity and are ready to pounce on it, criticizing the corporate world as soon as they have the notion that their world has been invaded. Your company needs to develop a relationship with this audience. That's what two-way communication is all about. You declare, they respond, you answer, they comment, you respond, they suggest, you confirm, and so on.

So if you're looking to understand the cost of involvement, look no further. Social media, properly executed, should be considered a part of your company's formal communication strategy indefinitely. This is one area I would not suggest "testing." It's an area that *needs* to be part of every company's operations and shouldn't be viewed as a promotional device only. The impact of social media should be felt by Marketing, Customer Service, Operations and Public Relations to be successfully integrated. What this ends up costing you financially depends on how efficiently you integrate this into your regular operations. Without supportive internal integration, I would not suggest social media campaigns of any kind. A company executing an effective campaign will generate discussion that will need to be addressed; otherwise it is an old-fashioned, one-way communication which defeats the purpose.

With so many communities and forums, it can be a daunting task to decide where to have presence and where not to. Take a look at the aggregate audience demographics and determine the tool most of your consumers would be using. Some communities skew toward the younger demographic, while there are other communities that focus around professionals with a significant household income (HHI). Picking the right forum to spend time on will keep your focus streamlined with your company placed where your customers can be found.

After determining your set of social sites in which to have a presence, whether it be MySpace, YouTube, Facebook, Twitter, or even Google Groups, it's time to appoint the appropriate areas of your company internally to engage your audience. Two "types" of interaction will be needed to sustain your social media objectives:

1. *Social and Customer Service Interaction*
    Once you're set up and begin your campaign to garner admirers and fans, constant service interaction will be required in order to engage your audience in real-time conversation. This interaction

is expected, especially in large companies today. Users who join in and participate will want to see a response from your company. Stale social media pages and Web sites aren't any fun and actually downplay your legitimacy. Once the social environment is executed, you should not turn it off.

2. *Content*

Fans and admirers of your product or brand will be stimulated with any content or "insider info" they can get about your company. Being the first to know about a new product or exclusive promotion can gain more awareness and possibly a viral message. Content won't need to be expensive or high-quality. Anything that gives your outside world an insider's view is appreciated. Be true to providing real information to your audience. Social media strategies that incorporate too many promotions will be viewed as nothing more than marketing ploys by your admirers, potentially turning them off. Always keep in mind that social communities gravitate toward content that "adds to" their experience or helps them in some way. Feel free to purchase a few digital video recorders and cameras and distribute them to a publicist, product manager or even a customer service representative. You will be happily surprised by the content these areas can come up with. Everyone provides a unique perspective on your products and services while sharing a common mission statement. Everyone, therefore, can and should be considered a potential "content producer" for your social media efforts.

The amount of money you decide to budget toward this endeavor really depends on how entrenched you feel you need to be. Agencies will gladly take over these efforts, but is an external entity really going to be able to respond to your consumers the way an internal resource could? Social media can be started up with little or no upfront costs, with most social sites and pages free to create and manage. The real cost will be found in the *soft cost* of internal resources being used to manage this process. Time to engage your audience will be tasked upon personnel taking over your social media initiatives. How much time they spend can depend on the number of interactions in a day, your industry, their workload with other projects and the number of social media outlets you have chosen to use.

You may want to allocate a small amount to a social media advertising campaign announcing your presence and inviting fans to join in. It's in the same fashion you may have created strategies to obtain email addresses for your email marketing campaigns in the past. Facebook has an excellent ad campaign program where your message can be perpetuated by the users if it is compelling enough, thus adding to your impressions and audience.

Once again, keep in mind that the more you make your social media strategy part of regular day-to-day operations, the more affordable you'll find it to be without significantly impacting your advertising/marketing budget. The following is an example of social media operations flow that can be incorporated within an existing company structure.

Social Media (Operations Diagram)

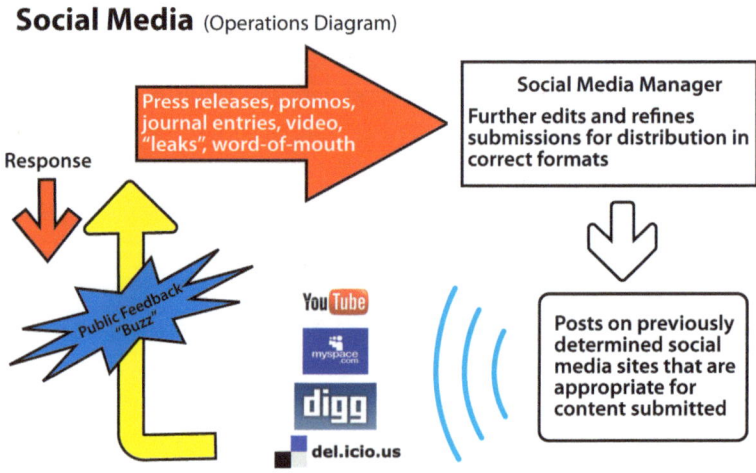

Response

Press releases, promos, journal entries, video, "leaks", word-of-mouth

Social Media Manager
Further edits and refines submissions for distribution in correct formats

Public Feedback "Buzz"

You Tube
myspace.com
digg
del.icio.us

Posts on previously determined social media sites that are appropriate for content submitted

ROI and Expectation

So, here we are with another assessment needed for our return on our investment. The ROI inherent within social media activity can depend on your motive for entering this space to begin with. Undoubtedly, your goals should be summarized by the following objectives:

- To build more brand awareness
- To engage your avid fans and build "buzz"
- To possess an aggregate audience of influencers
- To create unique and exclusive promotions
- To help control your company's public image

When it comes to a financial association of social media and the bottom-line revenue we are all responsible for, social media is far from instant gratification. Just like a new Web site, it will take time to build your supportive audience through daily management and content creation. Once this has been accomplished and is at an optimal level of participants, special promotions and offers will be the most direct way to assess how much purchase power your followers can have.

In speaking with a number of marketers around this topic, they all admit that revenue from this area can't necessarily be measured directly. These are fans of your product and brand. They are influencers and opinion leaders in their own circles and speak positively about your company. These external conversations (word of mouth) are valuable in their own right - more valuable in fact than the direct/immediate response you are looking for.

You may decide to float an offer to your social media members which generates $10,000 in sales. But realistically in some situations, over time, that number could be multiplied by 10. The conversational environment, insider information and engaged commentary all work together to build a landscape of users who will perpetuate your purpose and add to your bottom line. I consider social media audiences to be more "sensitive" in the sense that they are involved with two-way communications with your company and freely express their opinions and attitudes. Unlike Web site users, this group is *engaged* and looking to *actively participate* as you make them feel welcomed.

Take a quick look at automakers and how they use social media to build brand loyalty. Car companies know that their product on the Web simply isn't a click-and-buy commodity. They have built extensive consumer behavior models around the entire consumer-purchase process. Social media plays a strong role in both the pre- and post-purchase phases. The forums created and subsequent buzz assist those researching not only a car's features but the satisfaction of the owners. After the customer makes their purchase decision, they feel they are part of this community of satisfied, happy owners which they, in turn, convey to their peers. BMW's Mini Cooper is a perfect example of community development and stimulation.

If you can't use long-term purchase cycles to justify your initiative and have to use direct response, there are several things to keep in mind as you attempt to strike gold.

> - Create exclusive offers. Your social media fans and brand admirers should be handled as if they are made of gold. A cheap offer or basic discount that you would offer anyone online isn't going to be viewed as something special for them. In fact, it may cost you a few points of brand intent. Make your promotion truly an offer for those you know help contribute to your overall branding goals.

> - At first, only seek to justify your social media costs. The reason for this is because a program that pays for itself is acceptable most of the time if there are long-term returns applicable. Social media and

word-of-mouth marketing work hand in hand. If your promotions garner enough revenue to offset your costs (whether they be hard or soft), then you should consider it a profitable venture as your fans carry your positive value to their peers, adding to your bottom line in the long run. If you've made back what you spent, the probability is 99 percent you are profitable because of second-tier conversation.

- Place a value on each fan acquired. With each promotion you run, take the total revenue and back it into your total fan base. Revenue / Users = Fan Value. You can then use this to evaluate future costs of acquisition campaigns in terms of your social media member growth rate.

- Do not use tagged URLs or encoded links to track your revenue. These long strings of characters within a link scream "commercial." Interactive marketers today have adopted URL redirection services such as TinyURL to make offers more visually acceptable and not so obnoxious. Your tracking URL fed through one of these services yields a much shorter (and easier to remember) text link that the social media audience will find more acceptable.

Prepare Thyself for Truthfulness

You and your company should be aware that this two-way fan appreciation communication often yields critiques, negative comments and not-so-fun interactions. If you have ventured into social media for the right reasons, this will be seen as an opportunity to control your company's image and customers' perceptions. Some organizations would rather not hear the negative feedback or even try to ignore an adverse post, hoping people won't see it. The truth is that everyone involved in your company's social circle *will* see it and be waiting for a comment.

When opening a two-way communication medium, you have to be prepared for both good and bad feedback. More often than not, people tend to talk negative more than positive. It's a part of human nature that can't be explained, but it is a reality. Ignoring this type of feedback will do more damage than good, especially if it is within your own social media community. Handling the comment quickly and attempting to satisfy the user will only aid in your legitimacy with the rest of the audience. Sometimes the answer is quick and easy. Other times you may want to consult customer service or public relations. Either way, the important factor is handling it quickly and appropriately.

Today's scripting technology has allowed us to search and find postings outside our realm. The postings can be monitored for buzz about a new product or experiences with your brand. Several free services that can be found to search postings about your company or product are Trendrr, BackType, Social Mention, or Twitter. Paid services that are fairly inexpensive and can also draw associations and offer influencer data are Radian6, BuzzLogic and Trustworthy.

US Online Social Network Users, 2008-2013 (millions and % of Internet users)

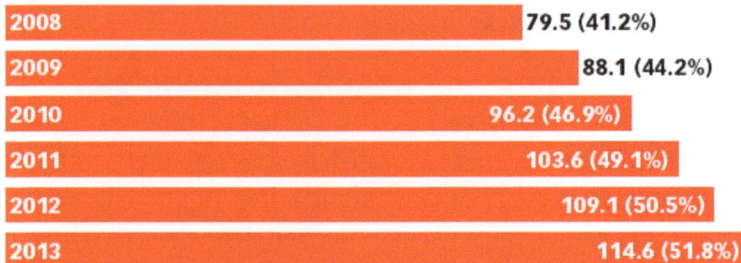

Year	Value
2008	79.5 (41.2%)
2009	88.1 (44.2%)
2010	96.2 (46.9%)
2011	103.6 (49.1%)
2012	109.1 (50.5%)
2013	114.6 (51.8%)

Note: ages 3+; use at least monthly
Source: eMarketer, February 2009

101290   www.eMarketer.com

Blogging Campaigns

If you feel you need to reach further beyond your realm to start the buzz, blogging campaigns can be very effective. Again, we're talking about two-way interaction with a sophisticated audience (no matter how old they are). This is an area all companies should venture into carefully. If executed the wrong way, the campaign can backfire and work against you. However, a properly seeded blogging campaign can work wonders for your awareness initiatives.

While you can always begin blogging and initiate posts on your own with internal resources, there are companies that can post messaging across thousands of forums within a short amount of time. Paid blogging campaigns also generate useful reports and provide insight into customer perceptions about your brand, product or service. This data is invaluable when planning your next interactions within social media.

A typical blogging campaign begins with your buzz initiative. This may be pointing out a new product or promotion to the social media audience. Perhaps you want to begin building public expectation about a new release. Once you have defined your goal and constructed the message, you are ready to begin your blogging campaign.

The second step is to identify blogs, message boards and chat rooms where your target audience is engaged. They must be 100 percent relevant to your industry or around a general topic associated with your services. Compiling a list of locations where your potential consumers are engaged will help keep you on track as you begin to seed the public forums.

Next, you begin your campaign. Engage the audiences through a conversational tone. Too many interactive marketers make the mistake of simply posting their offer expecting everyone to take notice and begin clicking. The context of the placement should come across naturally and organically in order to fit into the environment. Good blogging agencies are able to post within these natural settings quickly, sparking conversation amongst thousands of users.

After your posts, a thorough analysis should be assessed to determine the effectiveness. Revisit your postings on message boards and view the comments and expressions made by the audience. "I'll check it out" or "Looks good to me" are obviously indications of the response you are looking for.

Blog Marketing Code of Ethics

In 2004 I made a trip to Los Angeles to meet a blogging agency. At the time this was still a controversial space. After all, no one really had a lot of respect for a company or brand that *pays* people to talk about their offerings. But I've always been open to new ideas or approaches to marketing so I felt I'd go out and visit. To my surprise, I discovered that major brand names were already using this tactic to seed the online audience. Word-of-mouth-marketing code of ethics and best practices were still in their infancy compared to what we adhere to today. Back then, users weren't privy to the online conversations they were having with company marketers and simply thought they were an unbiased third-party user.

I have to say, I was astounded at the number of politicians and Fortune 500 companies that were already using this space. The agency I visited shared with me some of their past clients who had used their services to generate buzz messaging and discussion amongst the public at large. Both Republican and Democrat parties were using it to gain support for upcoming elections. Candy and toy companies were using it to stimulate sales around a particular brand from the stay-at-home-mom audience.

TV shows and movie studios were using it to attract more offline audiences. I was floored.

David Reis, CEO of DEI Worldwide, met with me and began discussion around word-of-mouth marketing. "Blogging" was a term that was still just beginning to catch on (although I had first heard it years prior). So the entire conversation revolved around social influencing, as we called it. Naturally I had a ton of questions that David was able to answer confidently, as the agency had been open for about two years. My feelings were stuck on the ethics behind paying users to speak about your brand and influence other users on your behalf. My primary concern was that I felt that contractors getting paid to engage in conversation were underhanded.

The initial response from David to this concern was, "Why?"

I told him that it was because they were hired to market a product in public forums. To which he asked me, "Isn't that what you yourself, as a marketer, get paid for?"

Then I reached a little further and explained that a contractor, posing as a *user* didn't seem ethical because the other party wasn't aware of this. He smiled and said, "Okay, so it's really about the anonymity of the contractor. Is that what you're saying?"

"Yes, I guess so."

"That simple word - 'anonymity' - is what separates positive and negative ethics in marketing via social influence," he said. He went on to explain that the world of online word-of-mouth marketing is engulfed in conversation around this very topic. Thankfully, he continued by explaining this aspect called for a code of ethics he was working to develop in order to gain a better position for marketers to take when engaging in these tactics.

Come to find out, David was a founding member of WOMMA, the Word of Mouth Marketing Association.

He knew he was in the early stages of a major trend marketers would take in the future as they attempted to harness the power of social influence online. In order for his business to succeed, he needed marketers like me to feel comfortable using these services. One of the primary differences that separated their agency from others was that his representatives clearly identified themselves as someone who "worked with" the company they spoke of. In the end being honest really didn't deter online conversationalists from reading and responding positively to the product or brand being promoted.

It is this degree of separation in your intent, no matter how small it may seem, that contributes to your overall success in blogging campaigns. For years I've lectured on the importance of realizing that the Internet (and any interactive media for that matter) holds *reciprocity* as a primary characteristic. What you put "out there" comes back to you. If you have SPAMmed, scammed, promoted a misperception, or falsely advertised, you are in for a world of karma. Everything you write, post, advertise and promote needs to have basic, universal, human integrity. I've also discovered that this was the one common teaching amongst almost every religion in the world. "Treat others as you want to be treated."

David then asked me to join him as they started a new campaign for one of their clients. He led me to a room with seven T1 lines that were directly connected to a cluster of five terminals. The room was full of employees ranging in age from their early to late 20s. One of his operation managers stepped up in front of a large whiteboard with everyone's attention. He wrote down the client's messaging objective and defined the target audience. Once he completed the direction for everyone, the sound of fingertips furiously typing away at the terminals was deafening. Within minutes, conversational marketing had started on the Internet, and I was comfortable with how those conversations were happening. To this day I'm thankful for this particular introduction to online social influence, as David's company still takes a truthful and ethical approach to their practice. Other marketer tactics that weren't so straightforward with online audiences have suffered major repercussions. Since I've been mostly employed by big brands, it probably saved me a lot of headache in my career to put the best foot forward in this area.

Since then I've used blog marketing when needed to accomplish specific campaign goals in the social media world. The WOMMA code of ethics has been invaluable for developing company policies and protocols when it comes to having employees engage this playing field.

The following is a summary of the WOMMA code of ethics, which can be adopted for any company's internal policy or procedure when working within social media. The most recent updates can be found on www.womma.org. I strongly suggest this is used as a well-communicated internal foundation for all companies integrating these tactics into their overall marketing strategy.

The WOMMA Ethics Code (EDITOR'S NOTE: Original punctuation and capitalization style have been retained from original source and not adapted to the style of the rest of this manuscript.)

1. Consumer protection and respect are paramount

We respect and promote practices that abide by an understanding that the consumer – not the marketer – is fundamentally in charge, in control, and dictates the terms of the consumer-marketer relationship. We go above and beyond to ensure that consumers are protected at all times.

2. The Honesty ROI: Honesty of Relationship, Opinion, and Identity

Honesty of Relationship

* We practice openness about the relationship between consumers, advocates, and marketers. We encourage word of mouth advocates to disclose their relationship with marketers in their communications with other consumers. We don't tell them specifically what to say, but we do instruct them to be open and honest about any relationship with a marketer and about any products or incentives that they may have received.

* We stand against shill and undercover marketing, whereby people are paid to make recommendations without disclosing their relationship with the marketer.

* We comply with FTC regulations that state: "When there exists a connection between the endorser and the seller of the advertised product which might materially affect the weight or credibility of the endorsement (i.e., the connection is not reasonably expected by the audience) such connection must be fully disclosed."

Honesty of Opinion

* We never tell consumers what to say. People form their own honest opinions, and they decide what to tell others. We provide information, we empower them to share, and we facilitate the process — but the fundamental communication must be based on the consumers' personal beliefs.

* We comply with FTC regulations regarding testimonials and endorsements, specifically: "Endorsements must always reflect the honest opinions, findings, beliefs, or experience of the endorser. Furthermore, they may not contain any representations which would be deceptive, or could not be substantiated if made directly by the advertiser."

Chapter V
The Future of Search

Honesty of Identity

* Clear disclosure of identity is vital to establishing trust and credibility. We do not blur identification in a manner that might confuse or mislead consumers as to the true identity of the individual with whom they are communicating, or instruct or imply that others should do so.

* Campaign organizers should monitor and enforce disclosure of identity. Manner of disclosure can be flexible, based on the context of the communication. Explicit disclosure is not required for an obviously fictional character, but would be required for an artificial identity or corporate representative that could be mistaken for an average consumer.

* We comply with FTC regulations regarding identity in endorsements that state: "Advertisements presenting endorsements by what are represented, directly or by implication, to be "actual consumers" should utilize actual consumers, in both the audio and video or clearly and conspicuously disclose that the persons in such advertisements are not actual consumers of the advertised product."

* Campaign organizers will disclose their involvement in a campaign when asked by consumers or the media. We will provide contact information upon request.

3. We respect the rules of the venue

We respect the rights of any online or offline communications venue (such as a web site, blog, discussion forum, traditional media, live setting, etc.) to create and enforce its rules as it sees fit. We never create campaigns or encourage behavior that would violate or disrespect those rules.

4. We manage relationships with minors responsibly

* We believe that working with minors in word of mouth marketing programs carries important ethical obligations, responsibility, and sensitivity.

* We stand against the inclusion of children under the age of 13 in any word of mouth marketing program.

* We comply with all applicable laws dealing with minors and marketing, including COPPA and regulations regarding age restrictions for particular products.

* We ensure that all of our campaigns comply with existing media-specific rules regarding children, such as day-part restrictions.

5. We promote honest downstream communications

Recognizing that we cannot control what real people say or how a message will be presented after multiple generations of conversation, we promote the Honesty ROI in downstream communications. In the context of each program, we instruct advocates about ethical communications and we never instruct or imply that they should engage in any behavior that violates the terms of this code.

6. We protect privacy and permission

We respect the privacy of consumers at all times. All word of mouth marketing programs should be structured using the highest privacy, opt-in, and permission standards, and we comply with all relevant regulations. Any personally identifiable information gathered from consumers through their participation in word of mouth marketing programs should be used only in the confines of that particular program, unless the consumer voluntarily gives us permission to use it for other purposes.

Is Social Media Public Relations or Marketing?

When newcomers to this space ask me what area the social media responsibility should rest within, it is usually between Public Relations and Marketing. I've been in numerous debates and discussions trying to argue both sides. Naturally when you reach a stalemate, two distinct answers emerge.

The first answer is the easiest. Public relations is a *part* of marketing. Marketing is anything a company does to obtain customers and start a relationship with them. PR is part of the relationship building in communications with specific audiences. Therefore, whether managed by PR personnel or not, social media is still part of marketing.

The flipside is that social media has enough ingredients from both marketing and public relations to be considered its own category. Pushing products or services plus managing a company's reputation and positioning are actions performed as a result of both PR and marketing initiatives. It wouldn't be fair to consider these influences as just one or the other, as both sides can take advantage of these tactics to meet their objectives.

Perhaps social media would be better termed as "social marketing" or "social relations," if it absolutely had to be categorized in one particular area. The interactivity of this playground begs to evolve into a whole new sector of business communication. My feeling is that since this space is growing as quickly as it is, with more and more resources within companies being dedicated to the practice, companies today would be smart in setting social media as a distinguished, separate vertical within their organizations.

If public relations were to take sole ownership of social media we would have a lot of very informed fans of our product and/or service. But that is all it would be without the promotional component. Marketing and promoting your company through social media is necessary to gain some sort of financial return on investment. When it's all said and done, it's the bottom line that counts. The thicker the line between a particular tactic and subsequent revenue, the more supportive senior management is of your cause.

Likewise, if all you do is continuously bombard your fan base with offers, discounts, promotions, contests, etc., you'll reveal the "commercial" side of your intentions and will soon be looking at a fraction of retained users. The unique content, insider information and proper messaging for your company is what PR brings to the table that helps balance the force of your intentions. Public relations softens the communication while marketing ensures the returns necessary to keep social media on course for positive bottom-line contribution.

Undeniably, Internet marketers have found a major ROI refuge in search engine marketing (SEM). For more than a decade, search engines have supported our online marketing budgets, yielding higher returns on conversions over any other tactic. Slight modifications in the advertising opportunities have been made over time, but for the most part the placement protocols have remained the same.

SEM encompasses both paid and organic placements. Search engine optimization (SEO) generally refers to the treatments made to a Web site in order to rank well within search results that are not "paid" (organic). Paid placements are typically made available using cost-per-click (CPC) models. Marketers bid on different search terms, proposing how much they are willing to pay for clicks on their listings.

These principles are the same as they were when search marketing was first introduced in the mid-'90s. It's remarkable that, over the years, this standard area of high returns has not progressed much in the way of the advertising model. Even so, search marketing to-date has been the best foundation to incorporate into online media plans with a revenue focus.

More than $10 billion a year is spent using search engine marketing strategies. Some companies dedicate millions of dollars toward this effort to ensure they are in the presence of users looking for them or the products and services they carry. The understanding of this practice is fairly common amongst Internet marketers, as it took a decade of conferences, research and well-known figures like Danny Sullivan to bring a common understanding amongst marketers today.

This chapter won't focus on search engine strategies or tactics. There are plenty of Web sites and books dedicated to educating the online marketer about how they can use this media channel to foster online sales. Instead, we'll look at the history of search engines, search marketing today, the long tail of search, and what the future of search will look like in years to come.

A Historic Review

Before the days of the big three search engines (Google, Yahoo! and MSN's LiveSearch), search engines started as primitive databases of Web sites indexed and searchable by title. These old indexes only allowed users to navigate by the name of a page or its title and weren't very effective for research. In 1994 WebCrawler entered the scene and was notably the first "full text" search engine, allowing users to search any word on a Web page that was housed in its database.

Soon after, other engines such as Lycos, InfoSeek, and AltaVista walked in, as their primary objective was to acquire as many dedicated users as possible. Yahoo! introduced a search engine that was also navigated by using directories, but the primary method users continued to employ was the utilization of keywords. By this time, the dotcom "bubble" was in full swing and many search engines found their way to popularity with investors looking to own a piece of these fast-growing tools.

In the middle of the bubble, in the year 2000, Google emerged as a more simplistic interface that used pagerank as a way to compose its search algorithm based on other pages that link to those the user is searching for. This methodology of determining the most appropriate search results has carried Google to be the number-one search engine today. Yahoo! composed their search tool through a myriad of acquired technologies they made from 2000-2003. LiveSearch by MSN emerged around the same time.

The Inner Workings of Search Engines

A common misperception is that search engines scour the Web for the information you are looking for instantaneously. In actuality the service is combing through billions of pages that are dynamically assigned a rank order to provide as a list of results. The process to obtain and display this list to you happens in three phases:

1) Acquisition
More commonly known as "Web crawling," search engines compose automated "bots" or "spiders" to follow link after link after link throughout this gigantic mountain of Web pages. SEO professionals are masters at ensuring your Web site is found and crawled on a regular basis. There are several rules to follow that have been around since search engines first started appearing on the Web. These same rules apply today, more than 10 years later, and should be a foundation for all your SEO efforts. There are a ton of companies that claim they have discovered the right combination of tactics to use, but your best bet, as an overview in this area, is to ensure your site has the following characteristics:

- *Relevant content feeding the spiders plenty of text that is rich with keywords you want to rank well for. Remember, "Content is king."*

- *Text links throughout the Web site (including your navigation) that link to other pages and deep link from your content*

- *Keywords in your page title that describe the page*

- *Appropriate description metatags in your HTML that use keywords found in your content*

- *Inbound links from other Web sites sourced within appropriate third-party content*

- *Frequently updated content which exhibits an "active" Web page*

There's no way to "fool" the spiders into collecting data off of your Web site and thinking it covers different topics than it really does or that it is more important than other Web pages. "Cloaking," "spamdexing" and "keyword stuffing" are some of the tactics used in the past to rank better, but from what I've seen it's simply not worth the time and effort to fool a search engine. Besides, working under the rule of reciprocity, it's not a realm to delve into. You are better off creating rich content that is valuable to your audience and appropriately touting it using the methods above for good search results. Again, these rules have been in place for over a decade and still stand today. You don't need to read too much into the search arena for your own purposes unless you are a professional SEO marketer. First practice these basic guidelines, AND THEN seek the advice of a professional.

2) Storage and Indexing
After the spider returns the page information to the search engine, it is analyzed using more scripts or algorithms. Specific, pertinent information that a search engine deems valuable is extracted and compiled for later retrieval. This information could be anything from keywords and metatags to image/graphic alt tags and bolded text. Or it can be, and in most cases is, a combination of these and other characteristics.

The results of the analysis are then stored within an indexed database for later retrieval. The analysis provides a specific assessment for that page and ultimately determines the "order" in which the index should appear subsequent to a particular search query.

3) Searching
When an actual search query is performed by a user, the search engine sifts through the database of indexed pages to provide a list of results. By using the assessment for each page, it quickly determines what results should be displayed in order to best match the user's search. The time search engines invest into their algorithms that assign the rank to a page is astounding. If you think about it, searches can be very subjective. A general search for "Las Vegas" might be done because someone is looking for hotel deals, whereas another person may be searching for restaurants. The search engine's goal is to try and make the results as relevant as possible to the user so they retain their audience.

Fortunately, online users are very mature by now in how they use search compared to 10 years ago. They have learned to search more specifically so the need to rank well under a general topic such as "Las Vegas" might not be as important as ranking for a query such as "best hotel rates in Las Vegas." When optimizing your pages, it will serve you well to target keywords as specific as possible to gain a qualified audience rather than take the shotgun blast "catch-all" approach.

Meta-search

There is another type of search tool available, besides the conventional search engine that should be mentioned. Meta-search tools differ from the dynamics of the actual search exercise. They submit your search to a number of search engines and compile an aggregated results list for the user. Meta-search can be more efficient for users in the sense that it is scouring multiple databases in real time.

This type of search tool is often more popular for specific interest verticals than general user queries. Industry-specific searches such as travel, entertainment and autos have their own meta-search engines available for users. This keeps the results list more specific on a particular segment rather than the world at large.

In some cases, the databases that meta-search engines extract information from aren't limited to other search engines. They may be from aggregator Web sites around a particular topic. This is an area of opportunity often missed by online marketing professionals simply because it involves XML feeds and other technicalities that are difficult to explain and present. If you are an online/advertising professional in charge of a Web site that indexes information about other products and services in your industry, I highly suggest looking further into meta-search and running a few trials.

A New Perspective

Now that we've covered some history and inner workings of search engines, we can attempt to look into the future at how search and subsequent search marketing will *evolve*. Millions of Web searches are conducted every day by millions of Web users who are maturing more and more in using technology to manage their daily lives. As new products and services are born we notice the audience gravitating to what they consider to be useful, more efficient and applicable to them.

This will undoubtedly change the search engine approach to audience and will undoubtedly change how marketers use search as a part of their interactive strategy. Search engines changing their approach to the online audience holds major implications for how we construct our Web pages and adjust our SEO practices. In the immediate future, everything is status quo. But all major search engines depend on audience, with advertising revenue as their number-one profit center. They know that the key to survival is audience retention, just like any other Web publisher out there. Without audience, there is no advertising inventory to sell to us.

Tapping into Behavior
As mentioned previously, search queries can often be subjective. What one user is looking for may entail a completely different intention than another user. With millions of people online, presenting a custom list of results for the individual is the Holy Grail, ensuring they get what they are looking for.

Search engine programmers and development specialists can write as many algorithms as they want in order to put together the "perfect" index for you and me when we do a search. Unfortunately, it will all be based on a common denominator, taking into consideration what the "average" person is looking for when they search "x."

Ultimately, it is our behavior that needs to be assessed in order to provide results that are customized and relevant to us. Behavioral targeting has been around for ages but typically only with regard to Web marketing. Users can be tracked after visiting Web sites with the advertisers presenting messages that are relevant for them. Remarketing to responders is also popular, where users who have visited your site or purchased your product online are re-messaged to in order to upsell or upgrade services. The ROI on behavioral targeting is fairly high as this practice gains more and more ground within online advertising budgets.

Most search engines have yet to tie into the same behavioral targeting offered through display advertising networks, but they are getting closer. But what about *beyond* just our Web behavior? What other things do consumers do besides surf the Web to review topics of interest or new products to purchase? More specifically, what do consumers do *in other interactive channels* that exhibits behavior that search engines would feel is relevant to include in results?

The answer is "everything." If you took a collective look at all my interactive *actions* over 72 hours, you'd be able to clearly see what my next purchase will probably be. Knowing that behavioral targeting on the Web generates substantial ROI, it's not difficult to see how ROI can increase even more with other layers of actions such as:

- Users calling certain 800 numbers or 411/information for specific business numbers as well as their texting behavior using predefined keywords

- Social media users posting comments or information about a particular brand or product

- Interactive TV and Video on Demand (VOD) allowing viewers to select shows and movies categorized within a specific genre. Commercials are already starting to use "A", "B" and "C" options on the remote for viewers to learn more.

- Frequent GPS usage for a certain area and locations visited

- Streaming radio stations and music selections also exhibiting preferences

- Credit card transactions for clothing, dining, entertainment, etc.

- Game consoles accessed to do more than just play video games, such as incorporating community, commerce and the rest of household entertainment

We certainly live in a digital age with everything that *could be* tracked and recorded for later marketing use. It is not far-fetched to say that search engines can interpolate and cross-tabulate these data to achieve their objective of making searches relevant for you, me and our next-door neighbors. For now this is simply a *futuristic* look at behavioral targeting that could be integrated into Web searches.

Before I go any further, let me say that consumer privacy is a topic I sincerely hope we continue to adhere to. We learned from the earlier years of adware, spyware and advertising trojans that in the long run, the infringement of user privacy can lead to disastrous legal implications. This is another instance where *Internet reciprocity* should be considered. If your company infringes on the privacy of users, even if it is a *perceived* infringement, you're asking for nothing but trouble. We all look for the optimal method of targeting behavior, but media technology companies will have to keep themselves in check every step of the way when acquiring new behavioral data.

That said, I believe that privacy in the future will be presented as "user preferences." If we truly use media to manage our daily lives, a certain level of "preference" will have to be established. Thus, you will have to give up a portion of your *consumer privacy* to reap the benefits that interactive services of the future can offer when presenting relevancy in what you are looking for. Permission-based marketing is a concept as old as Internet marketing itself, but you will see it modified to fit a consumer preference model. For marketers chomping at the bit, don't worry. Things are moving at such a rapid pace I can assure you, we are almost there.

Recommendation vs. Results
Search has always been about "search results" for particular queries. By taking into consideration individual preferences and needs, you will see the results evolve into "recommendations." This takes into the consideration individual user desires and personalizes their search experience.

The future of Web content continuously revolves around individual expectations, needs, preferences and interests. Search will be no different as developers look for any way they can to have a leg up on their competition by providing the best "recommendations" for their users. Until this point, all we've looked at is the Web as a behavioral tracking medium. Once things move beyond that, our searches as consumers will become even more relevant.

This shouldn't have a big impact on how you target people using SEO or SEM tactics. However, it should be a good glimpse at what online users of the future will be expecting when it comes to customization. Analytics and content management systems (CMS) are already offering options for services that adjust your Web site according to each and every user's behavior and click patterns.

Again, it's about putting yourself in the consumer's shoes. Consumers today are used to having the privileged access to media where, when and how they want to. As marketers, it's our goal to integrate our company, products and services into this environment; making ourselves available at every turn at the best possible time.

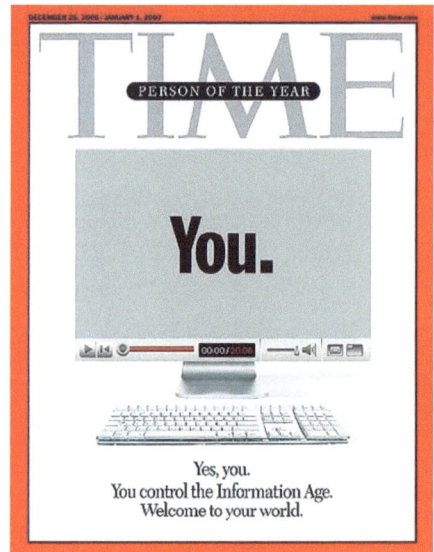

Yes, you.
You control the Information Age.
Welcome to your world.

The most evident display of this positioning to the masses was in *Time* magazine's Person of the Year issue in 2006: "You." The caption reads "You. Yes, you. You control the Information Age. Welcome to your world." The media is telling users that they own consumer technology. Thus, we shouldn't expect them to desire anything less than media that caters to their needs specifically. Emerging media infuses this into the two-way communication environment, making it another element that sets the next generation of media technologies apart from traditional mass media. Consumer customization and personalization are the primary overtones to your emerging media success.

Mobile Search

Mobile marketing will be discussed later, but I think it is important to point out that, while more and more wireless application protocol (WAP) sites are being developed to serve content on your cell phone browser, mobile search will continue to gain in popularity. Today, optimizing your mobile Web site isn't much different than your regular Web site. However, the intricacies of mobile search might change. Search engines will need to adapt themselves for mobile use as users are on the rise. Therefore, they will continue to modify and test search and indexing algorithms that are specifically for mobile users.

For example, you can see how the search query language and keywords might change just by observing how mobile users apply text messaging shorthand. Shortcut words and acronyms such as "PZA" may play a role in someone's mobile search for "Pizza". Obviously, if mobile is following the same optimization rules for now as regular Web sites, this acronym would need to be included in your content and metatags.

Social Media and Search

As more and more blogging takes place online with strings of discussion, your consumers are leveraging the opinions and advice of others in their purchase decisions. While the behavior of the online audience used to tool the search engines as a research resource, they are not seeking the input of other users who have purchased the same item. Your involvement with social media indirectly plays a role in your own SEO tactics. Blogs and posted comments are indexed as well. A positive presence will play a key role in the purchase decision process.

Prior to the mass practice of blogging, the inbound link practice of SEO was limited to link exchanges, link farms (not recommended) and a few message board postings here and there. Today, blogs give search marketers a whole new avenue of creating inbound links through blogging campaigns and individual influence postings. There's nothing like one of your satisfied customers posting a link of where they purchased your product or service.

Video and Audio Search

Companies are now taking a crack at spidering and indexing video content for search. Through the use of phonetic technology, search engines that offer up video and audio content results (recommendations) will soon be widespread. Once this occurs, it will make sense to ensure that all your video postings incorporate SEO as well. Keywords used during advertising scripts or voiceovers will be necessary for those looking to attain high rankings. Ambient noise will need to be eliminated and background music used strategically.

Currently there are only a handful of companies employing this technology, such as Blinx.com. The future holds phonetic search as a strong contender to help search engines differentiate themselves from their competitors. Although most of the video search engines are small today, you can rest assured they and their technology will be bought and intertwined with the major search engines of today.

As you work toward building content for your social media efforts and other applications for online users to engage with your brand, you would be well-served by taking into consideration the future of video search. Composing video now, with phonetic search in mind, will assist you later on. Imagine all the companies out there that create hundreds of videos, only to find out they aren't optimized for the future of our search world!

Search ROI and Application Outlook

The ROI of search marketing as a component to your overall online media plan is monumental. This is why search plays such a huge role in everything we do online today. The top search engines will continue to upgrade and modify their technology to ensure the majority of online users continue to engage their services. Advertising budgets spent on search every year will continue to grow so long as the technology continues to adapt to our ever-changing search habits online.

US Search Engine Marketing Spending, by Type, 2008-2013 (millions)

	2008	2009	2010	2011	2012	2013
Paid search advertising	$7,700	$8,925	$10,175	$11,525	$13,230	$14,725
Contextual advertising	$2,150	$2,450	$2,725	$2,975	$3,325	$3,600
Paid inclusion	$841	$910	$980	$1,052	$1,131	$1,205
Search advertising subtotal	**$10,691**	**$12,285**	**$13,880**	**$15,552**	**$17,686**	**$19,530**
Search engine optimization (SEO)	$1,550	$1,825	$2,100	$2,550	$3,200	$3,850
Search marketing total	**$12,541**	**$14,110**	**$15,980**	**$18,102**	**$20,886**	**$23,380**

Note: numbers may not add up to total due to rounding
Source: eMarketer, February 2009

Search shows no sign of slowing down and should be a top priority for marketers seeking online sales to substantiate their activities. Often times I've seen online marketing campaigns exploring many different emerging channels only to discover that the overall returns they achieve from search placements justify placements in other lower-performing interactive media while they ramp up their efforts.

If it wasn't for search, many online advertisers would be hard-pressed to test and trial the early adoption of new media. For instance, if your overall goals (or company objective) of your online search efforts need to return $5 for everyone $1 you spend (20 percent exp/rev) and you find that your search placements by themselves actually yield 5 percent exp/rev (gaining $20 for every $1 spent), then this allows the extra 15 percent to be absorbed by new media testing that may not perform as well.

It's vital to continue to monitor, tweak and adjust your SEM efforts. As new search placement opportunities are published by search engines, they should all be tested on a limited basis. Google's mission statement includes "...to organize the world's information and make it universally accessible and useful." The Web will continue to be spidered in the foreseeable future across all digital media. Let it be video, audio or even graphics, it is the ultimate goal of most search engines to make sure they index it and make it searchable. Thus, everything we produce, develop, publish or broadcast in any digital medium should be created with this in mind.

As our search marketing world is reshaped, test as necessary. There have been plenty of new offerings that crash and burn with advertisers. But search, just like everything else, will need to be regularly tested in order to strike gold.

Chapter VI

Mobile and Proximity Marketing

For the first time, in 2008, there were more text messages than phone calls using mobile devices. This is a huge milestone for society as it simply exclaims a coming-of-age for consumer use of this new form of media. There are thousands of marketers literally jumping out of their seats with anticipation for mobile marketing to take root and sprout into a new medium to incorporate into company strategy.

As with all emerging media, the same prerequisite stands - the number of users engaging this media must be large enough to justify a portion of budgets. 2008-2010 are my observations to be the years of testing. By 2011, mobile marketing will be in full swing and should come of age by 2016. There are a number of factors that have held US marketers at bay while we wait for acclimation within the population. Teenagers and "20-somethings" have adopted this new media as quickly as new technology is available. All the tools are in place for everyone to surf, communicate and purchase using their cell phones. Unfortunately, we are still in a period of waiting for that additional core demographic of 35-54 year-olds to get comfortable with mobile.

Behind the Curve

The US and European population is largely viewed as "behind the curve" when it comes to mobile adaptation. Specifically when compared to Asia. Asia's population of mobile users is massive. If anyone has the opportunity to visit, they will quickly notice the culture employing cell phones more frequently than their use of purses and wallets. Cell phones are a way of life and are truly used to manage their individual experiences. Research suggests a number of reasons the Asian culture has gravitated to mobile applications so quickly and on such a large scale:

- Personal computers and Internet access for everyone is rare. Asians have learned to use cell phones for tasks, whereas most of us are more familiar with PCs

- Email is the number one task we use the Internet for. Email usage emerged at the same pace of consumer connectivity in years past. Since most Asians didn't have personal computers, mobile was the only way most of them had to send/receive email and text messages. And we all know how much time we consume using email on a daily basis.

- Asia-Pacific countries have government influence on their mobile services. Typically, there are only a few primary service providers in any country, so they don't have as many options when it comes to using a particular service. The providers have freely released technologies as they have come available.

- The sheer population of mobile users alone helps the adaptation of capabilities grow at an astronomical rate. There are more than 1.4 billion subscribers in the Asia-Pacific region. China alone accounts for one out of every two text messages sent worldwide with more than 500 million mobile users.

- The cost of mobile and SMS services is very affordable, almost insignificant.

- Asian culture integration of mobile services goes well beyond the basic call and texting features. Financing, ecommerce and even religious functionality are frequently accessed. Direction finders are mobile applications claiming their own territory in the religion niche by pointing in the direction of Mecca for Muslim daily prayers.

The functionality of a mobile device in these countries goes way beyond what we are used to in the US. The first cell phone was introduced in 1983 by Motorola, but by the time they were widespread, personal computers had also flooded the market. Therefore, in the past we have always viewed them as *phones*. Europeans and Asian don't even refer to them as "phones," which has a single-utility connotation. Everybody calls them "mobiles" because they do so much more than talk.

US consumers have also been limited by the availability of cell phones that can actually tap into the features of wireless technology. Old Nokia phones in the early '90s had the appeal of being compact in size. A few years later, companies such as Motorola and Sony Ericsson contributed new models that allowed the users to text other phones as well as incorporate PDA-like features such as appointments and digital document reading. Earlier this decade consumers started to gravitate to the idea of "smartphones," which have become the standard for today. The mobile business has now attracted non-industry-focused companies such as Google and Apple who have developed their own models for consumers. Most users are accustomed to accessing the services these companies provide on a computer, but their introduction into the marketplace has been the catalyst consumers have needed in order to push user adaptation ... which can now be considered *explosive*.

The trend toward using your mobile device as a management tool has finally been adopted by US consumers on a massive scale. The audience is

there - ready to be addressed by marketers today.
A few limitations to the comfort level of certain users still
exist, but we are only a few years away from complete
entrenchment.

Mobile Phone and SMS Statistics

Before reading further, stop and consider the following...

- In 2009, the CIA World Fact Book reported that if
  each citizen carried one mobile phone, there are
  enough phones in use to accommodate 88% of
  the population. This is reflected by most European
  countries.

- According to The Mobile Marketing Association and
  cultural surveys, 80% of US mobile subscribers use
  text messaging. 75% of SMS users are just under 40
  years old.

- Over 3 million Americans will use mobile banking by
  2010.

- By the end of 2008, Marriott guests booked over $2
  million in room nights (source: Marriott International
  2008 Annual Report).

- eMarketer reports that US advertisers will spend over
  $1 billion in mobile advertising by 2012

SMS Strategy Implementation

To integrate mobile marketing into your company
strategy will require a small up-front investment as well as
100-percent support from upper management. I say *full
support* because this is an area that will be a significant
part of marketing plans in the future, and the more you
embrace it, the better off your company will be. There is
no in-between when it comes to mobile marketing. Either

you engage the practice or you don't. Simply dabbling along the way won't yield the future returns you should be expecting. This, of course, is once you've decided your product or service is applicable for the mobile channel, which will be discussed later in this chapter.

The mobile marketing environment can best be compared to a company starting a Web site for the first time. There are elements that are a direct likeness to your traditional online activity:

Online			Mobile
Web site	-	-	WAP site
Email addresses	-	-	Mobile numbers
Email campaigns	-	-	SMS texting
Banner ads	-	-	Banner ads
Publisher network	-	-	Mobile site network
Ecommerce	-	-	Mobile commerce
Domain names	-	-	Short codes
Micro-sites	-	-	Applications

Currently, there are a handful of mobile advertising "networks" out there that are pitching marketers left and right to jump on this bandwagon. Before jumping into an ad campaign within these networks, you will need a *short code, a mobile marketing service provider and a WAP site.*

Short Code

A short code is an assigned number that designates you (your company) as the originator of any message's text to or from. Think of it as a domain name that you use for two-way communication to your audience. The short code is really a short number used for SMS (short message service) or MMS (multimedia message system) communication. They are only available on mobile devices and do not require an area code prefix. The short code is meant to be a number that is easily recollected by users. At the time of this writing, Wikipedia reports short codes as being used primarily as an added-value service, such as voting or ordering ringtones. By the time this book is published, I expect the Wikipedia entry to be updated to include a lot more.

Your company short code is very important in terms of what you want it to be and what is best to accomplish your goals. In the US, the numbers are five or six digits, but this varies country to country. Some companies have opted to select "vanity" numbers that correspond with alphabetic characters. For example, the vanity number "46835" spells out "H-O-T-E-L". Some marketers feel they can use this effectively in advertisement messaging such as "Text 'yes' to 'HOTEL' to find our best rates." The problem in doing this is that many PDAs today don't have traditional dial pads. Palm, iPhone, and BlackBerry, for instance, have keyboards where the numbers don't correspond to the letters the way they do traditionally:

Traditional Mobile Dialpad

Sample PDA Keyboard

Therefore, it's best to pick a number that is easy to remember. "22222" or "54321" or "10101" are numbers that are easy to remember and dial in. This is the number you will want to include in almost every advertising media you use, so choose wisely - to change it again after proliferating throughout your traditional advertisement messaging will be expensive.

You can apply for this individually, but it is recommended to do it through your mobile marketing service provider (next section) as they have already done this for many other clients and know the ins and outs. The cost to lease a short code will range from $500–$1500 per month, depending on who you buy it through. Make sure your company has the licensed right to the short code and that you have a direct contract with the CSCA (Common Short Code Administration).

Once you've applied for your short code, be prepared to wait three to four months for it to be registered within all the network services. AT&T, Verizon and T-Mobile are just a few of the networks you will need to accept your short code for service. Some wireless services take longer than others; just don't expect to start using your number right away.

Mobile Marketing Service Providers

Companies providing SMS services are sprouting up left and right. The company you choose to work with will depend on the scope of your mobile initiatives. Some companies offer a simple Web-based backend tool that provides the very basic of services. If you are just starting out and have a relatively new company, the simpler the better. If you are a larger company with an existing email and client list, you may want to seek a more robust solution. Most providers provide an API (application programming interface) that will allow you to "interconnect" your mobile number collection database with your email listserv.

Service providers can charge anywhere from $500–$3,000 per month, depending on how large your mobile number list is and how frequently you deploy messaging. To start, spend as little as possible for the services you need. Chances are you won't have a large number of mobile numbers ready to receive text messaging.

Most service providers offer a do-it-yourself Web-based backend campaign solution. It is very similar to email marketing software, but the logic behind the tasks is built into the usability. You'll find plenty of ways to "play" with your database of mobile subscribers, from contest tools to surveys, setting the timing of deployment and content. Parsing out individual area codes yields geographic messaging for companies that are based in multiple regions.

You can also set up your keywords to generate unique responses. This is an opportune way to track your acquisition efforts as each keyword can represent a specific medium or promotion you are using, illustrating the level of response.

WAP Site

Mobile users will want to learn more about your services or may require a lighter version of your Web site to review for potential purchasing. A WAP (wireless application protocol) is nothing more than a Web site created for mobile device access. A common misconception is that WAP sites are a major expense. More often than not, this should be your least expense as you pull these components together. WAP sites can be written in "XHTML," which is a slight modification to how developers use common HTML for Web sites today. Your WAP site might even be developed by your internal Web team, if you have those resources available. Outside of this, don't plan on spending a large amount of budget toward a basic WAP site with additional information about your products/services. If you plan on engaging actual mobile device commerce, you may be looking at a slight bump in your expenses.

What is "XHTML"?

As mentioned above, XHTML is a slight variation to HTML. Any HTML developer can easily adopt the rules necessary in order to achieve the XHTML language. XHTML simply stands for "eXtensible hypertext markup language." While we won't get into the specifics of each and every variation, it's important to review the differences to demonstrate the simplicity of this lingo. Chances are you aren't a developer (although I always encourage marketers to have some basic Web development experience). So this won't get too deep for the average reader …

XHTML tags and elements must be in <u>lowercase</u>.

> Formal HTML example: <BODY>
>
> XHTML modification: **<body>**

XHTML must have <u>properly nested tables</u>.

> Inside lists must be within **<li>** and **</li>** tags.

XHMTL must have <u>one root element</u>.

> Virtually the same document structure as HTML:
>
> > **<html>**
> >
> > **<head> … </head>**
> >
> > **<body> … </body>**

XHTML must always be <u>closed</u>.

> Tolerance is allowed in HTML:
> <p>subject line
> <p> another subject line
>
> But not in XHTML:
> <p>subject line**</p>**
> <p>another subject line**</p>**

Any Web developer should have no problem incorporating XHTML language into their regular HTML practices. Should you look to have transactions occurring on your WAP site, you can still have your developers build the front end and your *mobile marketing service provider* help out on the transactional coding.

Your existing Web site domain can easily redirect to a different page or content based on the user's device. By applying a user-agent script to your existing page's HTML, those visiting your Web site using a mobile device can quickly access the "lighter" version you've developed for this purpose.

Again, there are many variations and specifics with regard to XHTML development, but the modifications are fairly simple for anyone versed in HTML. The main point of this section is merely to convey that a WAP site should not be a significant portion of your budget, as any competent developer should be able to provide you with this.

Do You Need Mobile Marketing?

The answer to this question is dependant on a number of characteristics with regard to your product or service. In my opinion, *every* company will eventually need to use mobile marketing to some extent. You want to be accessible to everyone at any time. People today don't necessarily carry laptops around everywhere they go, but they are certain to have a cell phone with which they can browse just as easily.

If your company's focus is around a service, you can use mobile marketing to push people to call for assistance. Many service providers use SMS to highlight special features or topics they feel that users are looking for. If you are a publisher of content and want to retain users on a regular basis, setting up a simple feed that announces new content via texting might be one of your strategies.

The same goes for dinner reservations or night club entry. These are services that don't require shipping or postage or anything that is tangible. Incorporating mobile marketing into these types of situations is easy because fulfillment is based on communication and information.

Having an actual product to sell is a different game. If your product is easily consumed via the Web, such as stock market information or other subscription services, mobile marketing will open the doors to a whole new audience segment you can successfully market to. However, if you sell tangible products on the Web, you will need to make sure that a mobile commerce interface is something that your potential consumers will use. The WAP site you create will need to provide all the same information in a "lighter" format that's easily accessible. If you have an entire showcase of merchandise, it may make sense to only offer your hottest products on a WAP site, as users will want to browse, research and assess the characteristics of your product (size, shape, color, etc).

Just as you practice in the online environment, be sure your WAP pages are secure when it comes to user transactions. Keep in mind that mobile users, especially the older demo, aren't completely acclimated to buying products on their cell phones. Product marketing via mobile should be approached with plenty of testing (and retesting) in order to maximize your conversions.

It's been said that *everyone* should start employing mobile marketing tactics. However, there are undoubtedly readers out there who still feel they need to be conservative to some extent, which is perfectly natural. Putting all the aforementioned aside for a moment, there are ways to test this medium to first see if it's right for your company and your consumers.

If you are looking to test the waters for audience affinity for your product/service, most mobile marketing service providers have a short code all set for your trial. They will, in most cases, put together a makeshift WAP site for you to use as part of your contract with them. This cost would be incorporated into your overall service agreement. You can use their short code in your promotional messaging and observe the reaction of your audience. Most of the SMS messaging or mobile network advertising would be a simple call to action using a unique, trackable phone number for users to call.

Be forewarned though, using one particular short code number for your potential consumers to opt-into will require you to "re-opt" them into your new short code should you decide to move forward and get your own.

Mobile Advertising and User Acquisition

Building a database of mobile users is critical to your longevity and ultimate goal achievement to turn mobile efforts into bottom-line revenue. As mentioned before, your mobile short code will need to be incorporated into all advertising - both online and offline. Using your short code in as many places as possible, including your own Web site, will be critical in building your database. Without a strong list of interested users, you will be hard-pressed to generate conversions in the mobile arena.

I, as well as other mobile marketers, have found mobile user acquisitions to actually be *easier in many cases* than gaining subscribers to our email newsletters. The CANSPAM act has made it more cumbersome to acquire opt-ins than mobile numbers ... for now. Texting to your short code is a quick two-way interaction that people can do on the move. A computer terminal isn't required, and it's easy for someone to observe your message ... "text 'join' to 44321" ... and quickly become a participant in your mobile community.

Unfortunately, the mobile marketing sector doesn't allow "lists" of mobile users to be accessed or leased like email addresses. Mobile marketing service providers are very stringent when it comes to the assurance your mobile user has truly *opted-in* to receive your SMS messages. Back in the early days of email marketing, lists were traded and purchased as easily as addresses for direct mail. After a few years, SPAM became a big issue to deal with, hence the reason for the CANSPAM act. Mobile marketing is recognized as an emerging medium, but applying learnings from the past, it's not a "free-for-all." A lot of time, dedication and money is spent acquiring a sizeable mobile list, so be prepared to invest in this area should you decide it is applicable to your business.

From my personal experience, the best way to increase the number of your subscribers in the shortest amount of time is to advertise within mobile ad networks, use acquisition messaging on your Web site, and introduce your new mobile community through your social media channels. These are the first steps to take, as offline advertising can take time to rotate in a text call-to-action. Once you've saturated both your online and offline opportunities with text call-to-action messaging, you'll see your subscriber list grow on a daily basis.

Communicating With Your Subscribers

Prior to delving into any SMS strategy, all marketers should review the Mobile Marketing Association's policies, guidelines and best practices to ensure they are in compliance. Reviewing these articles will save a lot of headaches in the future rather than taking the learn-as-you-go approach.

Once your mobile users have opted in, you will want to send them appropriate, meaningful communication on a regular basis. Of course all of us would love to send them promo after promo, but in reality they are looking to be part of a special group of people who have special privileges. You will want to engage this audience with quick news tidbits, interactive trivia or special insights that the general public doesn't have. This keeps your users enthused and reminded that they *belong* to your community of insider circles.

If you choose to constantly send promotional, retail messaging, then your list of mobile users will experience a drop off and all the hard work and budget you've put toward the acquisitions will be in the gutter. If you are an online retailer, send them announcements about new products or product features. But don't bombard them with two-for-one deals every day unless this is the core reason your audience has subscribed.

Proper SMS marketing takes just as much planning as email marketing campaigns, except it seems that the mobile community requires a little more strategy and involvement than just a blanket message you may put in your email. The rewards can be great in terms of conversions; just be sure to give them incentive to stay subscribed. *Contribute* to their needs.

Proximity Marketing – Bluetooth®

Proximity marketing is the distribution of promotions or messages to users of devices that have the capability to receive them along with their individual permissions. It can be applied through GPS-enabled devices, cell phones in a particular cell, or via a Bluetooth or WiFi device within a certain distance of a transmitter. For the purposes of this chapter, we will focus exclusively on the Bluetooth method, which is most commonly used and seems to be the faster growing area today.

History

The origin of the Bluetooth name actually goes back many years to Harald Blåtönn who served as king of Norway and Denmark from 935–985AD; the nickname

"Blátönn" meaning *bluetooth* or *shy tooth,* which implies the resistance to conflict. One of King Harald's goals over his lifetime was to unite ancient European tribes into one kingdom. The objective of Bluetooth is the same - merging multi-varied communication technologies into one universal protocol or standard. The Bluetooth logo was therefore designed from the Medieval and Germanic runes for his Latin initials (HB) by overlaying the two characters Hagall and Berkanan over each other.

Hagall - "H"   Berkanan - "B"   Bluetooth®

Bluetooth uses a globally unlicensed short-range radio frequency bandwidth. Data transmitted is spliced into packets and pushed on up to 79 different frequencies. When the technology was developed it was created for device communication within a short range at low power consumption. Unlike infrared transmissions, the devices don't have to be within line-of-site and can be far apart depending on the strength of the signal.

The most prevalent usage of Bluetooth technology is for hands-free communication through mobile devices, game consoles using wireless controllers, PC networking, PC interface devices such as the keyboard and mouse, and sending small advertisements in proximity marketing applications. Bluetooth technology will continue to grow along with the consumer need for wireless communications.

Implementation and Bluecasting

Servers using Bluetooth communications can connect with consumers using Bluetooth-enabled cell phones and PDAs. Pedestrians walking through a designated area can be reached up to 300 feet on most servers today.

The servers employ the use of a "dongle," which enables them to broadcast specific messages, small videos or graphics at the marketer's discretion. Smaller, more compact "hotspots" can even be carried by individuals, broadcasting up to 100 feet, making it a good application for street promotion.

Marketers can place a Bluetooth server virtually anywhere based on their size. Penetration success will depend on the number of individuals setting their Bluetooth reception to "on." Nightclubs use it to push special events happening inside. Outdoor advertising uses it to interact with passersby. Kiosks inside shopping malls use it to alert shoppers to special offers. The list of possibilities is endless, as you can observe the use of Bluecasting today in hotels, restaurants, museums, airports, train stations, stadiums, cinemas, concert venues, exhibitions and more.

The expenses involved are relatively affordable. It will depend greatly on the services you use to set up your network. Some may charge a setup fee, with a monthly cost afterward. Costs vary widely as new companies are seeking a level playing ground with competitive cost comparisons. I've personally seen networks costing anywhere from $1,500–$3,000 for setup and as low as $300/month.

One of the drawbacks to Bluecasting is the number of users who don't have their Bluetooth turned on to receive messaging. The results of engagement will also change based on how high the traffic density is in a particular location. There are a couple of additional tactics marketers can use to counteract this:

Signage: Place stanchion signs or posters that inform your audience that they are in a Bluetooth zone and can receive promotional messaging.

Message Size: Keep your messaging short and easy to receive or interact with. Transmissions of video and graphics can greatly impact the number of users who can connect at once along with the time it takes for downloading.

All communications to enabled mobile devices come with permissions. The user's cell phone or PDA will ask if they would like to receive communication from you, allowing the opt-in. Your Bluetooth marketing service provider may even give you a login for a Web-based tool that can change the messaging and any files you are transmitting at your discretion. This makes it easy to set daily offers or update graphics, ringtones and videos on the fly. It also allows you to do it remotely without having to go to each location needing an update.

Statistical Summary

Perhaps the best way to determine if Bluecasting is right for you is to review the statistics of users who have the capability of reception. Ultimately, there are a few signs that this media will still need a year or two to really get traction. But as fast as time goes by, you may decide it is something you should implement now.

Based on my own research and testing over 6 months within multiple commercial venues, I've concluded the following…

-   Over 90 percent of mobile device users in North America have Bluetooth capability

-   The default setting for Bluetooth is "always on"

- The default setting for *Bluetooth discovery* is "always off"

- Over 70 percent of mobile users have Bluetooth enabled

- Penetration of successful transmission is 13%

- Average opt-in rates to "receive a message" once transmitted is 95%

Bluecasting is becoming more and more an accepted method to reach consumers. The younger generation is especially tuned in to this approach as it will become a common part of their lifestyle over time. Statistics around the success of direct marketing campaigns at this time are relatively unknown as there have not been many case studies published for marketers to learn from. However, Bluetooth usage introduces a strong opportunity for us to acquire more users in our mobile community database for messaging later.

The main question to ask is if your target demographic "gets it." Products and servicing to an older audience may need to wait a few years before they adopt Bluecasting as *acceptable*. Perhaps this is why lower-costing services have found this as a means of promotion with an acceptable ROI, such as nightclubs and cinemas. In the meantime, using Bluecasting as an extension of your overall mobile marketing strategy will be a very useful practice, indeed.

Chapter VII
The Gamers

From the early '80s to the present, I have to admit my fascination and participation in video games is surpassed by very few people I've met. I remember Dad taking me on his lunch breaks to a local arcade featuring all the now-classic games, handing me a handful of quarters to explore while he continued his quest to get the highest score on Ms. Pac-Man. Although the technology was simple by today's standards, coin-op video games back then required huge housing cases to bring a few megabytes of data to a big screen for quarter-spending consumers to play.

When video games were first introduced, so were the stereotypes. The older generation simply didn't understand the fascination (and addiction) happening to a bunch of pimple-faced teenagers as arcade games moved over to home entertainment consoles. Unfortunately for me, that was where my parents drew the line. I was afforded no Atari or ColecoVision to pass the time. However, I found refuge as some of the neighborhood kids' parents allowed the taboo into the house where I enjoyed hours after school sitting in front of the television with my buddies. Hindsight says my folks made the right decision, though. They eventually bought me a home computer which I grew accustomed to using for more than playing video games.

In 1994 I was in my college dorm room studying for finals when one of my friends from down the hall popped his head in to say, "You gotta see this!" Ready for a break anyway, I followed him down to his room where his roommate was playing a game called "Doom." It was a shareware release from id Software that featured a first-person perspective of run-gun-shoot mentality. I didn't leave their room until six hours later.

For the next six years I re-engaged my interest in gaming and looked to purchase every new, hot PC title I could get my hands on. In 2001 I remember conceiving the idea around video games interpolated with advertising. I wrote a business plan around the distribution of advertising through multiplayer networks to see if there were any *takers*. I never found any. But fortunately this media has still evolved into a channel allowing marketers today to push their specific brand and messaging.

My own experience with video games allows me to completely shun the notion that it is only for the younger generation. While the youth of today still play video games as a pastime, yesterday's teenagers in the "video game introduction era" such as myself are now 35+ with full-time jobs, careers, money and net worth. It has since been my personal challenge to educate senior management with reservations of advertising in this arena based around stereotypes. The fact of the matter is, if you break down video games into the appropriate demographics that play them, there's little difference in audience comparison with most traditional media.

Not too long ago, "multiplayer" games were limited to PCs connected via a LAN line to the Internet. Today, the leading home entertainment consoles such as Xbox® 360 and PlayStation® are connected, allowing players to compete against other players worldwide in real time. Several companies have negotiated the rights to advertise in these games and offer in-game advertising as an optional part of our advertising media mix.

Gaming Demographics

If you think gamers follow the same stereotypes as the 80s, you're living in the dark ages. The fact is that most gamers today fit every demographic, psychographic and economic profile you can think of. Growing up in the 80s introduced us to the coin-op machines which are virtually out of business today as home entertainment consoles are providing an experience that is just as rewarding.

Truthfully, gamers are most likely me, you and everyone we know. If you are targeting men, gamers should be a first place you should look. It seems that every angle you approach, gamers are a huge audience that can satisfy your audience goals. Why else would Guitar Hero III beat Harry Potter and Lord of the Rings in sales during the first week of launch? (also the first game to top $1 billion, by the way)

Consider the sheer number of North American gamers and growth projection (in millions):

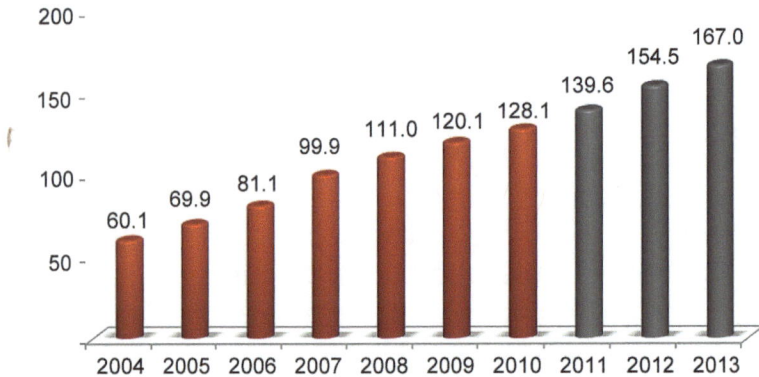

Now review the following statistics:

- Over 70% of males 18-34 own a game console at home.

- Males 18-34 in the US play video games 10 or more hours per week.

- Video game product sales are increasing approximately 12% year over year.

- 21% of adults play video games every day

- Over 30% of all money spent on entertainment is spent on video games.

Sources: Frank N. Magid Associates, 2008, The NPD Group / Retail Tracking Service 2008, Interpret GaMeasure 2008, The NPD Group / Entertainment Trends In America 2008

In-Game Advertising

Once you've evaluated in-game advertising opportunities, you'll find this world can be compared with *outdoor advertising*. Outdoor advertising uses daily effective circulation (DEC) metrics to convey how many people will drive by your billboard or walk past your duratran.

But there's a major difference in the way most in-game advertising networks validate impressions.

The impressions in in-game advertising are measured based on the percentage of the screen your branded advertisement occupies over time. For instance, an impression may count when your message takes up a predefined percentage of the screen for more than 10 seconds. This is extremely beneficial to the marketer as the measurement tolerance for adequate exposure is more than acceptable.

Offline outdoor media isn't able to measure this at all. Your best assessment of its effectiveness is to monitor the number of calls to an 800 number. In-game advertising uses actual metrics to qualify an impression, guaranteeing you get what you pay for. In addition, the cost of impressions within this media is closely compared to high-end Web site banner ad impressions, which can range from $20–$35 CPM (cost per thousand).

You can also geographically target and daypart your advertising. If you are a regionally based company, you may choose what ZIP codes receive your message. Messaging can be rotated based on time of day or during specific periods in a given month. It's almost as if outdoor advertising took on the dynamics found within the Web.

Today, home video game consoles don't allow very much opportunity for direct response. Your brand should appear bold with a simple message. Using 800 numbers and text call to action is perfectly acceptable but will generate a limited response. Bear in mind when players see your message they are in the middle of a game. They are already *engaged* in *activity* when they see your branded advertisement. Don't expect a direct response from these users while they see your brand flashing in front of their eyes in the middle of blasting enemies or trying to lap their racing contenders.

The best way to approach in-game advertising is to align it with your branding initiatives. Interpolate the audience with overall frequency and penetration goals you have for a new product or service modifications you are looking to communicate. Simpler is better when it comes to your message. Forget the idea you need to get direct response to warrant the effectiveness of this media. Its overall impact and positive attributes are inherent in *branding*. Granted, this isn't the easiest selling point to your senior management, but speaking to it in the same fashion that advertising agencies speak to outdoor advertising will help your cause. Faced with the demographics that are perfect for your brand, you can leverage the statistics to make a better case for your entry in this emerging media.

There should be some considerable thought toward your branding when engaging in-game advertising. Many titles on these advertising networks are for mature audiences only and involve graphic scenes of killing and slaughter. You should be familiar with the titles that are centered on this type of content and be proactive when selecting what games to appear in. Consumer products such as movies or music might not feel the need to be wary. However, other brands may find it more aligned with their company's brand attributes to advertise strictly within sports and racing games. Any well-established in-game advertising agency should be able to parse specific titles appropriate for your brand.

Losing the Stereotype

As the demographics exhibit, some of the most targeted qualifications of individuals can be found within in-game advertising. This is an example of media that hasn't been embraced by most companies because some of the demographic for some game titles can skew younger. You can avoid this younger demographic using day parting (advertising after 9pm, for example) as well as the titles you advertise within.

Older players between the ages of 25 and 34 spend around $700 per year on their video game activities. More recently in the face of a recession, it has been discovered that the number of hours per week and money spent on video games has *increased*.

Getting past the stereotypes will be your main concern as you look to expand your marketing efforts in this arena. It will most likely require a lot of discussion with management to get buy-in. But after using enough case studies, demographics, survey data, and presenting a plan to test your exposure, you should be able to sway the majority of opinions.

Placements

As previously mentioned, in-game advertising agencies use predefined metrics to achieve your branding objectives. Each gaming console has specific attributes that offer both in-game ads as well

as interface integration. The entertainment consoles have gravitated toward community as a way to foster perpetual use. Community boards, video downloads and messaging features are all part of this strategy. Oftentimes the game console manufacturer will allow your presence in this space as well. Sponsoring a special area or feature can also gain attention from the audience as gamers are intermittent in their game playing while they are in this interface.

The easiest way to place your brand is to advertise on the network much like a display ad campaign on the net within different Web sites. Each game in this network has specific placements designated by the game developers to be put in rotation. This may include billboards, building wraps, posters or even blimps. It all depends on the game itself and where it would make sense to have your advertising appear. In addition, these placements can be animated or full-fledged videos.

Another method of advertising in video games is a direct product insertion. While this requires months if not years of advance planning, it can gain unlimited audience that purchases the games. This is *not* part of a typical in-game advertising network. It arises out of a direct relationship between you and a video game publisher.

The best way to obtain product placement or sponsored advertising with a video game publisher is to contact the top developers themselves and pitch your idea. Your product must have relevance to a particular title they are developing or plan to develop in the future. Gaming industry publications often review games before they release or inform the public of new development releases. It would be wise to subscribe to a few of these monthly publications, find an appropriate game title in development, and contact the publisher.

Profit margins often run thin for game developers. This gives marketers an opportunity to pitch their company's product as potential content. With all the trademark and copyright obstacles out of the way, a product's in-game insertion is relatively easy so long as the game is in the development process. The key is *relevance*. Your product must make sense to be used as content within the game itself. Total cost can be negotiated between you and the game developer.

Creating a whole new advergame may be an option in itself. Advergames have gained in popularity over the years, and the right product combined with an appropriate experience can lead to massive exposure. In 2006 Burger King released a series of games produced in under a year that were sold at their restaurants for $3.99. Burger King's agency approached Microsoft with a proposal to produce and deliver these games for the Xbox and Xbox 360. The time it takes to develop one title can be two to three years, let alone that Burger King was requesting three of them to be produced within a year in time for the holidays. The result was a huge success that Burger King publicly claimed as a direct impact on quarterly earnings.

In Burger King's case, the titles imposed over $20 million in expenses to their budget, which apparently was well-spent money when evaluating the impact. However, advergames can cost under $20k depending on the format in which they are used. If you want a title that is sold as a packaged retail product, the costs can be in the millions. There are many boutique developers in the marketplace that can deliver an advergame unassociated with any gaming console as a standalone. Standalone video games can gain traction on the Web by themselves depending on content, playability and audience appeal.

If you feel your company's product or services would find appropriate audience within the video-gamer community, I would suggest sticking with in-game advertising networks or potentially developing a game for consoles, which will vary greatly in terms of cost. However, a standalone game can be effective when you are seeking a broader audience and can cost a lot less. In addition, a standalone advergame on the Web can be tracked and tied directly to revenue in your reporting. I've personally been involved with advergame projects costing less than $20,000 only to turn over $1 million in revenue within a year. Contrary to this, console video games and in-game advertising tactics have yet to prove a direct-response outcome.

What to Expect From Video Games in the Future

We've already noted that in-game advertising won't yield direct-response tracking to warrant placements seeking a direct ROI. As all media evolves, the video game console in today's households will also transform itself into more than just a gaming mechanism. Microsoft, for example, plans to use their Xbox 360 product as the first step toward facilitating an entertainment "hub" for the common consumer domiciles.

US In-Game Advertising Spending, by Segment, 2008-2013 (millions)

	2008	2009	2010	2011	2012	2013
Console- and PC-based	$117	$124	$140	$155	$167	$170
Web-based	$286	$319	$370	$418	$464	$511
Total	**$403**	**$443**	**$510**	**$574**	**$631**	**$681**

Note: excludes advergames and advertising on mobile games; numbers may not add up to total due to rounding
Source: eMarketer, June 2009

Today, the game console has started to intertwine music, video and DVD features that help make it a larger part of your home-based media entertainment than just video games. Soon you will see these consoles taking the place of your home stereo system and other components, making it a multi-functional necessity. Streaming music and video from a WiFi network will allow us to use one console instead of the age-old cumbersome task of switching between peripherals. Companies such as Microsoft are banking on the fact that using video game consoles is a natural step in this direction.

It makes sense to most consumers in the "plug-and-play" era to not be bothered with a bunch of settings, wires, and remote controls. The yearning for a single home entertainment component will naturally lead us to buying a gaming console whether we consider ourselves gamers or not. Direct access to your home computer will soon be available through these interfaces, along with full-functioning Web browsing on your big screen.

In-game advertising opportunities and functionality will therefore change as well. In the near future, gamers will not only be able to see and be *branded*, they will also be able to engage, experience and interact with the advertising presented in their games. The connectivity of all media combined with technological advancements in the interface will allow all users to quickly experience and browse through product offerings. In-game advertising strictly for branding purposes will be in the past as marketers find two-way communication during a user's gaming experience.

I mentioned before that we shouldn't expect to see gamers pick up the phone, text or email us when they see our advertising since they are in the middle of an activity. This statement is only made with regard to *today's* capabilities. If interactivity is introduced within our in-game advertising, it would stand to reason that gamers (who are used to interactivity in the first place) will take the time to peruse product offerings or brands they have an affinity for. Soon, we as "gamers," or we as "marketers," will be able to take advantage of a video game interface that will afford us the two-way communication environment necessary to conduct a transaction.

Once we reach this stage, in-game advertising will open a whole new world of opportunity for direct response. Users (gamers) will be able to *enter* an advertisement in a virtual realm, allowing them to visit our Web sites, interact with our branded products, and purchase via special promotions. Finally, outdoor advertising in the virtual sense will have the two-way communication needed to measure its true effectiveness.

The video game industry is developing at a rapid pace with the introduction of new gaming consoles every few years. Keeping tabs on this changing industry would be a good idea as more and more companies find an area of participation that services their marketing objectives. Personally, I can't wait.

Chapter VIII

Virtual Worlds

Playing video games is one thing. Actually living, communicating, buying, selling and getting married in the virtual space is another. I remember first hearing about Second Life in 2002 and looking it over not as an advertising channel but as a participant. Although I never *registered* an avatar, it soon popped up again in late 2006 as *the next big thing* in emerging media.

From August 2006 to February 2007, virtual worlds grabbed the attention of every digital marketer from coast to coast. Industry publications produced headlines that screamed the need to jump into this space based on the increasing number of users as well as platform capabilities. Conservatively, my colleagues and I watched as major brands such as Pontiac, Adidas, AOL, Dell and Reebok entered the virtual world and established their residence. After a short while, it was apparent that these brands were in for public education as the interactivity soon became the next headline.

The Virtual World Environment

Virtual worlds take a step beyond what was formerly known as a *gaming* experience and present real-world concepts in a virtual environment. Entropia Universe, There and Second Life have all brought the online world visual representations of a cyberspace nature. Commerce, real estate, advertising, residency, social groups and sports are all part of the virtual community that makes up the activities within virtual worlds. Virtual worlds boast that if it can be imagined, it can be done.

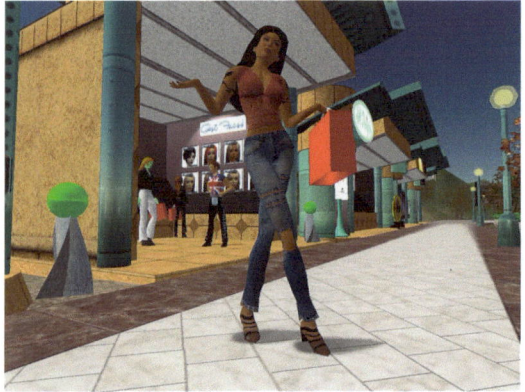

While Second Life is the dominating virtual world of today, it has yet to really prove adaptability and reliability for marketing professionals. From a capability standpoint, this is by no means their fault. It is the sheer participation from the virtual community at large. Marketers who have entered this area have been met with a number of challenges arising from our previous misconceptions about virtual worlds.

The virtual world *meta-verse* offers a unique audience looking to participate in social discussion and activities. Users range from all different age groups, demo- and psychographic profiles, as well as consumer behavioral attributes. Just as the Internet offers a wide range of consumer groups, virtual worlds also hold an audience which may be attractive to many companies.

Virtual worlds go beyond the two-way communication aspect, offering interactive exercises and events that have characteristics available to truly immerse one in a company's brand or product application. It is an environment where marketers can build models and real estate, with open doors to all users (visually represented as *avatars*).

From 2006 to 2007, there was an incredible spotlight placed on virtual words, with Second Life grabbing most of the media's attention. It appeared as though hundreds of thousands of people were joining as *residents* in these communities making them very attractive to advertising specialists. To be able to create a storefront where residents could virtually experience your products and make purchases was a goldmine on the surface. However, after a short time this appeared not to be the case.

For one thing, marketers weren't necessarily ready to contribute to communities. Everyone continues to be "stuck" in the days of one-way communication. While you may be able to get away with basic brand presence and call-to-action messaging in regular advertising, don't expect to continue this in the virtual world. As a participant, you are expected to *contribute* to the community at large. Offering tools, apparel, or added features that avatars find useful will aid you in your quest for positive engagement. Simply building a storefront with your brand on the sign out front won't garner the results you are looking for.

Secondly, be prepared for all types of interaction between you and the virtual world residents. "Griefing" is an action frequently taken against new corporate residents entering the world to advertise their wares and services. Described as a virtual form of terrorism, griefing can be in the form of an explosion, fire and brimstone

fallout, or targeting specific avatars to experience system crashes and connectivity degradation. Many virtual world residents don't take kindly to a corporate big-brand presence of any kind unless there is a needed and viable contribution present. They hold an adversity to the corporate presence and seek out tactics to make the lives of us marketers uncomfortable.

Finally, the virtual world commerce system doesn't necessarily translate to instant real-world sales. Depending on your product and its accessibility, you will need to determine if it has a place to embark on a storefront in virtual worlds. Most transactions occurring within this media are based on virtual-world dollars (in Second Life's case, "Linden Dollars"), which you will need to account for with an exchange rate in our third-dimensional reality for tax purposes.

Virtual worlds offer opportunity when used the right way. Keep in mind that most of the conventional rules of advertising and marketing are out the window when you establish a presence in virtual worlds. Engagement with the community is key. This isn't a media you can place and then sit back to see what happens. It is a tactic that requires constant involvement with unknown returns.

Level of Investment

Without much history it is difficult to predict where levels of investment should land in the future. Approaching this media should be done with caution based on hundreds of companies demonstrating failure within the first 18 months of entry. The primary question that interactive marketers should answer is exactly what their main

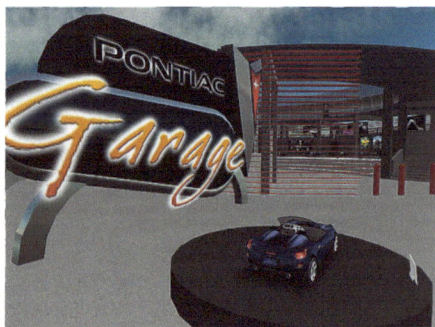

objective is. Again, this is back to basics, but as we see in all unknown emerging media and strategy, the basics are the best place to start.

It's best to keep in mind that virtual worlds are being used for more than just revenue-generating entities. They are useful for gauging public feedback with regard to new products and services. Avatars (users) are quick to develop opinion when they are within the presence of a branded entity or live representative. Traditional research methods may fall short in some areas that virtual worlds can make up for. For instance, studying consumer reactions as they engage with a new product often yearns for adjustments to the study on the fly such as color, options, etc (just as Pontiac was able to do with their car-driving experience). Virtual worlds allow marketers to do this and gain valuable feedback in a relatively short amount of time.

Whatever your intention is, usage fees are relatively cheap. Many virtual worlds are free to enter for basic services but for more advanced options and metrics insight, a premium charge (usually around $10–$20) will be incurred. In addition, residents of the world can buy land and build *virtually* anything they want, whether it is a storefront, statue or an *experience*. Land costs can be as high as $200 per month, which is still within an affordable range.

The real cost is incurred when it comes to development activity. Personally, I am not a virtual-world developer, nor do I feel my day-to-day business activities require me to have this skill. Hiring a specialist consultant or one of the growing number of development studios can be as expensive as necessary to accomplish what you want to build. Contracts can range from $5,000 to as high as $150,000 for your establishment.

Anyone can *learn* construction in virtual worlds. It's the same as educating yourself on building a Web site or becoming proficient with graphics software. The time you dedicate to acquiring programming skills will ultimately depend on your current business situation. If you are a small-business entrepreneur, you may have the time to acquire this skill and accomplish your vision of virtual-world presence. Thousands of residents in virtual worlds manage *micro-transaction* ventures where their products are anything from virtual clothing and pets to real estate and script purchasing.

Larger companies will more than likely opt for the outsourcing route. Careful research and planning with your development studio will be required prior to settling on an actual contracted scope of work. Marketers for large employers are usually tasked with managing a multitude of communication channels and won't have the time necessary to learn construction in this space.

Ultimately, your initial investment will be based on your objective(s). Additional funding *will be required* to ensure success in brand recognition and resident acclimation. After launching your project, users will begin their brand interactions with your company and services, quickly offering feedback; positive or negative. You will certainly spend more money tweaking and adjusting and possibly advertising your presence within the world. Marketing in a virtual world to residents can have associated placement costs or not, depending on the methods you wish to engage. After all, social media and vigilante assistance can exist in both reality and virtuality.

Virtual worlds are a developing space where there aren't any rules of engagement. But like most interactive media, there's a definite reciprocity inherent with your actions. Providing something unique, that is an added benefit or tool for the residents, will achieve the results you are looking for in acceptance with potential revenue following. Just having a brand presence with no opportunities for engagement or community interactivity will leave you high and dry, explaining your actions to company management. Many corporate endeavors have failed due to their entry centered on reasons such as the "cool factor" or because their trigger-happy choices are based on keeping up with the Jones'.

Many companies entered and abandoned virtual worlds because of their mistaken assessment that there was fault with the medium. A more precise reason behind most failures was that there was fault with their *message*.

Eyes on the Future

The companies that have made big entrances (and headlines) in virtual worlds as part of their marketing strategy did so largely because their original intent was not a focus on ROI. Unfortunately, most of these excursions ended in project abandonment. Consider these examples:

- American Apparel – Opened a virtual store in 2006, closed the store in 2007

- Reuters – Opened a media outpost in 2006, abandoned their facility in 2008

- Wells Fargo – Entered and left in the same year

- Starwood Hotels & Resorts – Established aloft presence in 2006, left in 2007

- AOL – Abandoned their virtual world presence to pursue a presence more conducive to instant messaging

- Mercedes – Launched presence and abandoned virtual world 13 months later

With these examples, it appears that big brands and marketing presence have no place in the virtual realm. Yet statistics show users continually increasing their personal entry with each passing year. In-Stat, a market intelligence company, predicts that by 2012, more than one billion registered users will exist in virtual worlds, yielding $3 billion in revenue for participating companies. This happens to be a very real example of how fast things can grow. It was only in 1997 that *total* online consumer spending reached $1 billion. Another trend analysis company, Gartner, predicts that over 70 percent of businesses will have some sort of presence in virtual worlds by 2012.

Conversely, other entities engaged the virtual world and found success. They had predefined objectives outlined and used their presence to enhance user experiences with their brand. Added revenues were derived

from fusion of the in-world environment with their offerings that contributed to the community. Some examples include:

- IBM Academy of Technology – Used a virtual world for a conference and annual company meeting. Estimated ROI in cost savings was more than $300,000.

- Coca-Cola – Established a formal partnership with There.com in 2007 offering unlimited branding opportunities through special events

- In 2008 Domino's Pizza invested heavily in a series of digital multi-channel retail platforms, including Second Life, with no plans to slow down any effort toward "client-facing" projects

- The University of Delaware provides an automated tour fly-through of the campus to attract new student prospects

And, by the way, these are just partial lists of the estimated 10,000 companies that had grabbed onto the fast growth of virtual worlds by 2006.

Perplexing, isn't it? How can a media have such a large and growing reach yet be so allusive to a standard business model?

During my research in uncovering the secret to successful marketing within virtual worlds, I ran across this comment posted on a WordPress by Michael Durwin. This single paragraph simplified the summary of opinions with regard to this discrepancy of usage and marketing failures. In one particular blog he states:

"A lot of people talk about American Apparel closing its store. It may have been one of the first but it was also one of the worst. There was [a] stage but no posting as to when fashions shows took place. AA clothes are for the most part non-descript. Why would it appeal to me to buy one of your plain t-shirts for my avatar? I have an alligator head and fairy wings! Not to mention that there was no staff at the store, no events, NOTHING of interest, oh, except the free 6 pack of beer on the desk."

Source: http://mdurwin.wordpress.com/2007/07/25/corporations-leave-second-life-we-never-knew-you-were-there/

Interestingly enough, users *are* still participating as residents *and* making money within virtual worlds. The question marketers have been asking themselves is how can *they* have presence for their companies and generate sufficient revenues to consider virtual worlds a viable form in their marketing channel mix. The first wave of companies launching their presence during the "hype" (2006–2008) failed miserably. Recapping the primary reasons for this (already discussed) combined with characteristics of the virtual world presents us with the following:

1) *Target Market Definition*
   Marketing in the virtual world is an entirely new demographic in itself. Conventional targeting that dictates race, age and sex is almost irrelevant when determining your strategy for entry. Virtual worlds allow anybody to be *anything* they want to be. Companies looking to target a specific parameter of demographic failed to realize this truth in virtuality.

2) *Environment Considerations*
   Many companies neglected to fully understand what can happen in an open-world free-reign environment. Proficient residents have capabilities to manipulate the world in many ways that may not be appreciated by big brands. Setting virtual fires to buildings or initiating protests with meteors crashing are unfortunately a potential occurrence that businesses should be aware of.

3) *Community*
   "Contribution" is of major importance. A branded presence alone isn't enough to bring in visitors. The community needs to have a *reason* or a *benefit* tied to interacting with your brand. A simple show and tell won't be enough to gain the respect and acceptance of the community. Providing tools, enhanced features or complimentary incentives will be a necessity.

4) *Lack of Research and Personal Experience*
   There was a huge misperception of marketers as they jumped on the virtual-world bandwagon. Reported resident numbers don't necessarily translate to regular users. Although virtual worlds

may report millions of registered participants, only a fraction of them may be logged in at any given time. Without much personal time spent on experience, marketers jumped in with both feet and found themselves having to face the reality of audience attraction (or lack thereof).

5) *ROI Goal Establishment*
Without an established road map toward success, many companies failed to justify their existence in virtual worlds without concrete metrics. Inadequate sales and lack of significant branding metrics didn't translate well to a direct contribution to bottom-line goals. This was a rudimentary oversight but was still doused by the overwhelming desire to do "what everybody else was doing."

6) *Technology*
Another contributing factor was the technology itself. With connection and processor speeds varying amongst users, it is difficult to maintain high refresh rates allowing a "smooth" interactive experience. In many cases users find themselves with a cumbersome amount of "lag" when more than 50–100 avatars were occupying the same location. Connection and processing speeds worldwide simply haven't caught up to the intense amount of data transfer involved with virtual-world experience. Companies found it difficult to communicate and display their business offerings.

Author's Advice

I have never pushed virtual worlds as a potential channel for effective communication and revenue as a contributor to the company's bottom line. That said, I don't think we can legitimately dismiss this media altogether. Virtual worlds continue to evolve. Although Second Life gained most of the attention during the bandwagon days,

There.com amongst other services continues to gain in popularity as well. My overall viewpoint on virtual worlds stems from the perspective of making enterprising returns (revenue) large enough to positively impact profit figures. Let's toss "branding" and "social media" to the side for a moment in order to identify hardcore value in generating sales.

Observations suggest that this may be another case of "*first* isn't always *best*." As we observe companies coming and going, the services are continuously adjusting what they offer to make sure they keep the residents they have while giving others reason to open a new account. Companies have spent a lot of time and money to venture into this frontier while giving onlookers (namely, their competitors) ideas and suggestions for best practices.

My advice is two-fold and is given largely based on the interactive marketer's situation. Do I think that Fortune 500 companies should go out and spend 10 percent of their budget on creating an interactive storefront in a virtual world? No. Do I think that small-time entrepreneurs should spend time creating the interface themselves to increase business? Yes.

Virtual worlds are a social networking and marketing medium that simply haven't demonstrated a profound commercial success. In lieu of this, smaller companies that have the time to invest on a presence with a shoestring budget can find many opportunities to grow their revenue. Big corporations have a number of factors working against them that ultimately equate to failure no matter what they do. However, the smaller entities have a clear shot at making their fortunes within the environment.

The key to virtual worlds is the community which inhabits them. You aren't going to drive your typical customer to visit you in the world. Shelving your standard demographics and opening yourself up to the community at large will have to be a conscious decision that a lot of companies won't want to do. After all, why go after a *possible* income stream littered with variables when you already have your traditional channels solid and producing what you need?

Virtual-community residents recognize big companies from small ones and tend to gravitate toward those that are the most innovative *and* contributing to their world. Small companies have the time to invest in order to learn the market, while larger corporations would rather outsource the work to an agency specializing in this space. The problem is that, even with a specialist, they still don't understand your business. This is also why many advertising agencies can be successful on the branding side of the fence yet fail when it comes to generating a strong ROI. No one knows their business like the people who work there.

When looking at small verses large business success, consider this example: a large Las Vegas casino/ resort wants to establish a presence in a virtual world by replicating their hotel and allowing users to virtually explore their offerings with the intention of offering real-time reservations for future stays. At the same time, a Las Vegas concierge service has a small plot of virtual land that offers the same thing, without the construction of a massive hotel. The smaller concierge representative also spends their day mingling around the world talking about their service and has multiple Web-based initiatives driving traffic to their in-world business. In my mind, the concierge wins based on their flexibility, un-intrusive presence and willingness to cultivate relationships. The big resort will fail because they will have nothing to *contribute* other than virtual construction users can walk through.

The virtual-world community is finicky. They don't want the influence of large companies in their domain that are seeking nothing more than revenue from their ventures. Hence, big brands are typically subject to *griefing* and other assaults emulating the residents' discontent. Large corporations will be better off creating a small business unit that can spend time establishing a presence in the virtual world in order to migrate the residents into acceptance rather than pushing their products and services all at once.

Virtual worlds have had their time in the spotlight as a trendy marketing venture, having since disappeared amongst the number of big-name company failures. As technology begins to catch up along with the younger generation posing a massive number of avid users, meta-verses should still be monitored. I believe that we haven't seen the last of the hype, fully expecting virtual worlds or virtual "somethings" to play a part in our advertising and marketing efforts in the future.

In the meantime, feel free to dabble, read case studies, test small ventures, and observe as an onlooker. Just beware of flying penis attacks.

Chapter IX

All About the Video

Possibly one of the biggest change that has occurred in advertising formats is our use of video and its capabilities. Every day you will witness video adaptation to different media channels while we are well beyond video being primarily a one-way format. Today we can interact, search, contribute and digest video across almost every media we consume. Three elements can be overviewed to provide a good perception of where we are now with video application, distribution, interactivity and composition.

1) For almost 50 years, video was confined to television with the emergence of basic recording formats such as VHS and beta tapes. Once the Internet was well-footed in the '90s, video made its way to online distribution. The proliferation of high-speed

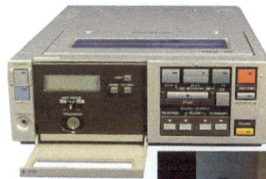

1982

2009

Ashton beats CNN in Twitter "followers"

was the launch pad that sent video distribution flying in every direction. It can now be viewed virtually anywhere, anytime, which has contributed to the massive change in how marketers use video today. Advertising "reach" was once limited by exclusively using television as the medium.

Now we are able to impose our video reach in multiple formats, making it cheaper and more efficient to use in order to get our message out to the consumer.

2) "Interactivity" has also fostered the change in the marketing usage of this format. Video segments can be *selected* and viewed as easily as turning a channel. Layering video with Microsoft's Silverlight™, Adobe® Flash® or other development software allows us to create hotspots and user options that can go as far as immersing the user into the context. Leveraging interactivity with video evokes an interactive experience with your product or brand like none other. As the introduction of interactivity only began a few years ago, more and more users are becoming accustomed to engage applications where they can manipulate, make choices, and ultimately manipulate video to their liking.

3) Video composition (or "production") has changed as well. Post-production (the work after the video was shot) used to be done in editing bays with extensive tools and flyers to edit your work. Countless hours were spent with the marketing professional and the producer barking comments and changes to the editor operating the system. Production bays are still being used today but most of what used to take hours to do can now be done much more quickly on a PC. This has given the new generation the capability to produce videos like a professional using freely available software. Production is cheaper, faster and more flexible. This aspect alone has grown video availability by leaps and bounds around countless topics.

I recently came to the conclusion that my kids will never know the meaning of "rewind." Video on demand has altered our lifestyle around television programming. Families are no longer gathering around the TV at a certain time to watch their favorite programs. They are now recorded using DVR, DirectTV and other products and services for us to view at a different time. In addition, this imposes a murky element to the definition of ratings and gross rating points typically used in offline advertising metrics. Advertisers have had to adjust around this as well, increasing the need for various tactics from product placement to television audience participation ("American Idol").

What Does It Mean to Have Reach?

With multiple forms of distribution, reach is a key metric that has evolved as well. The basic meaning has remained the same, but the perception and importance of it has changed based on the advertiser's usage of multiple video channels. The good news is that reach can be more easily calculated with online or digital distribution. The bad news is that the quality of reach has changed not necessarily based on the target audience but on overall impression.

Accuracy is in demand from every corner of every industry with an advertising objective. Online media has provided specific metrics and numbers that are measurable and dependable. Therefore, the screams for accuracy are heard from everyone in the marketing profession.

But just as traditional media used to "bake in" assumptions, we still find ourselves having to do this in the interactive world. Video may count 1,000 views in a day, but a percentage of those views weren't actually viewed. Web page placement below the fold, interruption or connectivity issues during consumption, and percentages of view are all factors that make our overall reach metrics compromised.

This can be counteracted with the cost of reach decreasing dramatically. The same reach that can be achieved spending $3 MM on a :30 spot during the Super Bowl can theoretically be obtained for less than a third of the cost over time using digital channels. The cost total of your reach can range from your $10 CPM in an online advertising campaign to a few thousand spent on production. If your video project is "viral," it can literally capture close to the same number of viewers for little or no cost at all.

Targeting specific demographics also counteracts reach fallacies through precision in delivery. Garnering 100,000 views won't mean anything if your target audience isn't present. It's okay to sacrifice half of your audience to make sure you are targeting the right audience segment. The tools available to marketers today allow them to focus on a reach that is qualified through appropriate targeting.

When Guitar Hero® III was published by Activision in fall 2007 millions of copies were sold to Xbox and rock-and-roll fans around the world. After a few weeks, the YouTube videos started coming in with different gamers submitting their talent for the public to see. I took notice of one in particular, which showed a group of college kids in a dorm room huddled around a television screen watching their roommate play the last song on the "expert" level. A fellow gamer sent this to me, which succeeded in humbling my own ability to play the game. At the time, there were 300,000 views. For the next few months I kept showing it to other people and looking at it to see how many views it had. After six months, it reached almost 10,000,000 total views. The video simply showed a college kid nailing almost every note for over eight minutes. What was this reach worth?

Another YouTube video that surfaced in my inbox during this time was one entitled "Where the Hell is Matt?". The video was only a few minutes in length but featured a guy named Matt Harding visiting more than 42 different countries, *dancing* with the residents of a particular city. After less than a year, the video had 20,000,000 views. At the end, five seconds were given to credits. The very last slate of the video said, "Special thanks to Stride® Gum for making this possible." What was *this* reach worth?

Where the Hell is Matt? (2008)

Antseranana, Madagascar

The Guitar Hero III video cost nothing to produce. It was a great plug for the game itself, but as far as what it did for Microsoft or Activision brands, there was very little acknowledgement to be had by the users, as there was no mention. "Where the Hell is Matt" was obviously sponsored by Stride Gum with a mention at the very end. The video probably cost a few hundred thousand dollars to travel, shoot and produce. But $300k seems like a drop in the bucket to achieve 20 million views (which is about one-fifth of the Super Bowl audience for 10 percent of the cost).

Granted, the Guitar Hero video was done by an independent party without any ties to Activision or Microsoft. But had Microsoft marketing capitalized on this from the beginning, there would probably have been more views and better brand equity, thus making it a good investment.

The Stride Gum video demonstrated someone's vision that materialized into one of the biggest viral videos of 2008. They witnessed Matt Harding's first video (with much smaller distribution) and reached out to him to help sponsor a second. The second one with their assistance gained almost twice as many views, pushing the Stride Gum brand. It was a terrific investment on their part and paid off extremely well in viewership.

One thing many companies forget is that their consumers are all equipped with the capabilities to produce video as easily as writing a critique or voicing disgruntlement. For those of you who market big brands, one thing to keep an eye out for is what your biggest *fans* are doing with your product. Some of them may currently be producing their own videos using your product from sheer adoration alone. Putting all brand standards and usage preferences aside, you will probably find their videos gaining significant views without any cost to you. Imagine what would happen if you used social networks to reach a particular consumer advocate and offered a small budget to help them pursue their goals just as Stride Gum did.

Of course, there will be instances where your brand isn't depicted the way you would want it to be (such as Mentos® being used to create geysers out of Diet Coke). Instead of taking a guarded approach, open yourself up to see video presence and distribution for what it is - a mega-opportunity to get your brand out there with little budget. You can always work to massage your brand presence in future productions. It's unfortunate, but I know too many marketers of Fortune 500 companies more concerned about brand usage than they are about the size of the audience witnessing the spectacle. This isn't to say that you should sponsor a production that trashes your image in the public eye. What I *am* saying is that we shouldn't let these concerns overshadow the presence of opportunity.

Get Used to It!

The presence of video evolvement has started and will continue for years in the future. Every six months, we will learn about new technologies taking advantage of video distribution and production. With the popularity of video communities such as YouTube, coupled with the emergence of television on demand, I honestly believe we will have channels available to us that are 100-percent interactive, allowing us as viewers to key up what we want. Channel surfing will be replaced by programming preference.

Several cable operators, such as Cox Enterprises (Cox Communications), already employ *selections* that can be accessed on your remote. To date, there have been few television campaigns taking advantage of this feature, but more and more advertisers will gravitate toward the value of user option. Commercials can engage viewers by offering several options as to what they want to see next and opt-in for more information to be sent to them. By involving the audience to the extent that you invite them to learn more about several different topics during your commercial, you essentially have an open invite to the sales pitch. Cable companies are struggling to obtain advertising interest in this feature, which is amazing. I find it difficult to understand why many marketers wouldn't take more advantage of this feature than they currently do. Perhaps it's because we are so used to interactivity only happening on the Web that we can't see the value in viewer options with digital television advertising.

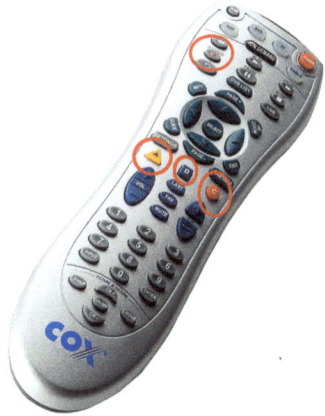

Digital television holds a huge untapped potential and will only evolve and exhibit even more opportunity as the years go by. Cable operators will learn better ways to communicate this offering, while marketers will learn how to utilize it for their objectives.

Online video communities are growing beyond the most optimistic expectations. Any segment of our lives can be shot on video and uploaded for the world to see within seconds. Just as message boards and image banks grew in the late '90s, video has now become the next generation of communal activity. Interactive marketers will continue to harness the power of distribution (both paid and free) to their benefit as more and more devices advance, from cell phones to portable media players.

Video distribution networks online have also grown to aggregate huge audiences. Video syndication across thousands of Web sites, evoking millions of views, offers marketers a great opportunity to present their products, services or brands for little cost. Many distribution networks offer video production, branded framework and social interaction as well to enhance both advertiser and consumer experience.

As offline television advances with digital formats and VOD, we'll start to see the capabilities we currently have on the Web introduced to our household living rooms. Interactive marketers will start to see video as more than just a presence— as an opportunity to engage the users through interactive choices, options and features. Currently the only way we, as consumers, have been approached was through company Web sites and applications where we can look for what we want and research prices, availability, etc. The future will bring consumers the ability to experience brands and product via video. Choosing what color you want, walking through an average day scenario, and even testing the different features in a simulator are all going to become common traits of customer engagement.

By 2010, over 50 percent of all online users will be consuming video. ***How will you engage them?***

Video Advertising

There are just as many ways to implement video into your interactive advertising plan as there are advertising techniques combined. This portion of the chapter is dedicated to the most popular and effective methods out there. The expense will commence with the tactic you use. Some are free; others can be pricey. It's been argued by offline marketers for years that television is the most effective method for advertising in terms of branding and direct response. I'd like to think of it as *video in general*.

First, let's start with video ad networks. There are many forms of distribution. You can have your own video distributed amongst different content and channels for the same cost as the CPM on your banner ads. Some networks allow integration with Flash making your video interactive, yet others don't. Depending on your product or service, you may find this distribution to be most effective. Take a look at what your company has done on television. Has it worked? Chances are you'll be able to use the same tactic via these networks with similar results for a fraction of the price.

If you've found a network that will allow you to overlay your video with Flash-integrated elements, all the better. Use this to your advantage and add interactive selections for more information or user controls that allow them to switch gears midstream and delve further into a particular touchpoint. Publishers call this interaction "hot spotting," and it can be very effective if you find the right audience.

Another cheap distribution method is to incorporate your video as pre-roll. Many video ad serving companies have partnered with publisher Web sites that offer video in a community format or as standalone content. Having your video distributed as pre-roll can be even more cost-effective than a video distribution exclusively. Again, it all depends on your product, objectives and budget.

The best form of pre-roll is the kind that users *don't mind* watching. Many times publishers give their users the option to "skip this ad," which you don't want them to do.

If it's pre-roll, you will only have a few seconds to get them interested and act on it if it is a direct-response initiative. Whenever dealing with pre-roll, the best acronym (as useful as it is ancient) is AIDA - Attention, Interest, Desire, and Action. If you want them to pick up the phone and call, place the number consistently throughout the video. If it's a click to a Web site you are looking for, make sure your domain is easy to remember. If you are simply branding a new movie coming out or a new service, then you can rest assured your message is being communicated very affordably.

Viral Video

I chose not to create a particular chapter about *viral* advertising simply because my take on what makes something viral may differ from many marketers out there. It can be very subjective. However, I think there is a lot of relevance in the viral aspect when it comes to video.

When answering the question, "What makes something viral?" try to answer the following:

- What makes something *funny?*

- What makes something *memorable?*

- What makes something that *compels you to share with others?*

- What makes something *you will watch more than once?*

- What makes something *unique?*

- What makes something that *provokes you to talk about?*

These questions sum up the answer to making a viral video (or any interactive development for that matter). The unfortunate side is many of the answers are subjective and unquantifiable. If interactive marketers were able to answer these questions, you would see more than "elf yourself" during the holiday season (www.elfyourself.com).

The viralness of a video can go a long way and obtain massive reach once it is distributed. Fortunately we have testing grounds such as YouTube to see how much it is handed from one user to another. If your video has enough viral energy behind it, it won't need much promotion to find your targets. Just be sure you have the proper messaging integrated, such as a call to action, to make sure you don't miss out on an opportunity.

The interactivity of your video itself is another viral component. Allowing users to mash up the stream, edit, or incorporate their own images and text at certain parts certainly lends itself to community attraction. Creating a viral video isn't easy, but that's why we have a multitude of creative studios ready to propose different ideas. Most studios will take the time to brainstorm these ideas on spec, with you doing little up front to incentivize them. Once a big idea is formulated, negotiate wisely, as sometimes the best ideas can turn out to be big disappointments.

Product Placement and Hot Spotting

"Product placement" is another strategy coming to pass that has helped marketers insert their brands into webisodes or online videos with little cost. This used to take a lot of advance planning and a lot of phone conversations. Sites such as Filmmortal.com offer community platforms that connect advertisers and brand executives with independent film/video developers for appropriate product insertion and placement. This has become more and more popular over the years since the initial days of BMWFilms.com and allows marketers unique opportunities to have their products and services presented to the public. Who knows? Perhaps there's an independent producer out there who has the next hot viral video ready for you to sponsor a product placement.

Aside from the benefit of creating an *emotional* connection to your product, product placement (also called "embedded marketing") provides a means for the producer to be funded to complete the movie. In the past, the overall impact to your brand had to be measured over time and wasn't very effective for direct response. With *hypervideo* capabilities (also known as "hot spotting"), marketers can make their product placement *clickable* for users to pause what they are watching and get more information.

Although hypervideo was first used a decade ago, it has taken a while for marketers to employ this tactic as a common practice. This stunted growth rate has been attributed to the time it has taken for broadband connection speed penetration. Nevertheless, today it is widely used and has proven to be an excellent way for users to experience your branded product in a contextual setting. *VideoClix* and *Klickable* are just a couple of software solutions that have made hypervideo development commercially available.

The future of hot spotting is still wide open. Full feature films and webisodes can potentially be created through the application of sponsored products by marketers wishing to have a more unique presence in the marketplace. In addition, your promotional videos, b-roll, :30spots or other content can utilize the power of hypervideo themselves if your product is multifaceted or contains a number of features.

For example, if you are a car manufacturer and want to demonstrate the unique characteristics of the design, video hot spotting can allow users to "explore" all features. Write and produce a short story or spot that provides viewpoints on all of the different characteristics.

Every time the camera brings into view one of these features, the overlay technology makes them clickable. The question is, "what next?" The answer is, "whatever you want." Once the user engages the hot spot, they can click through to a detailed information page, find a special offer, or even jump to another video that animates the feature and further explores the different components. The choices (and opportunities) are vast. Vast only *after* the user has discovered your video in the first place ....

Video Search Engine Optimization

Video search engine optimization (VSEO) and video search engine marketing (VSEM) will *soon* be as common as SEO and SEM are today. Currently, there are two types of video search engines. Those that look primarily at the metadata and text descriptions surrounding the video are considered first-generation and evaluate videos the same way as they would a Web site. The contextual placement of the video with links and text surrounding it bears impact on how relevant it is for search terms. Relevancy can still be hit-or-miss since the metadata can be misrepresented by stuffing keywords within the text or video title/metadata as well as other not-so-accurate treatments.

The newer video search (second generation) engines not only rely on metadata but the actual video content itself. Speech and visual recognition software coupled with optical character recognition (reading in-video text itself) allow the file to be deciphered and digested. Users searching for video with descriptors such as "Saturday

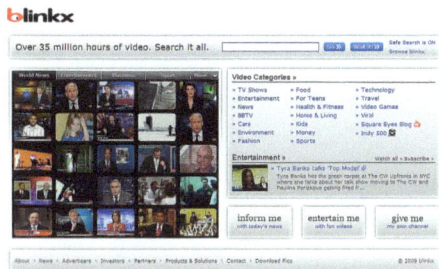

Night Live skit with cat" will be able to tap the search engine's resources and index for videos that contain that exact content.

Second-generation video search engines bring a whole new set of SEO rules to the table. Not only do metadata need to be applied after a video is produced, but the producers themselves need to take into consideration how the video will be *read*. Knowing that many search engine publishers are evaluating speech-to-text recognition software, a couple of considerations will be imperative during the video shooting and post-production editing process:

1) Background Noise: Interlacing a clean audio sound bite or voiceover will make it easier for the search software to recognize, pick up and associate specific words. If the video is shot with too much background noise, the voice might be un*readable* and thus ignored.

2) Scripting: When compiling the script for your video, be sure to use specific keywords that describe your overall project. For example, an actor who would normally say, "Here we are at the next event," might want to say something like, "Here we are at the **international motocross competition** watching the **distance jump** at the **Diamondback** race course in **New York**." Keywords spoken distinctly and clearly will add validity to the video, thus increasing your ranking in the results.

3) Imagery: Visual recognition is just as important as speech. Software that searches through video clips takes snapshots of different segments and associates them with a resource bank of millions of images. Though the accuracy is still questionable, it would make sense to use images that are clear and shot with good lighting.

4) Optical Character Recognition: Any in-video text - such as credits, closed-captioning or animated overlays - is considered as well through OCR. Just as we've been using OCR for years with desktop scanners, the same technology is being applied to video. Words that appear in-video can be deciphered and adopted as descriptors for the video content.

We are still a few years away from video search being perfected and exploding, but with each passing quarter it seems there is another breakthrough making video search more meaningful and relevant. While to some this may seem too forward-thinking to act on, I suggest it will be much easier to incorporate these practices now rather than wait. Imagine the expense a company will have to undergo in order to *re-shoot* or *re-edit* entire video banks of files just so they can rank well within video search engines. By keeping VSEO in the back of your mind when executing new projects, the emerging marketer side of you will ultimately save a lot of time and expense in the future.

3D Video

The first 3D movie I saw when I was a kid was "Creature From the Black Lagoon" re-issued for television in the 1970s. I recollect 7-11 convenience stores playing a big cross-promotional role with the 1954 film producers that were involved with the upcoming television special. Back then, it was a big deal that probably cost a significant amount, with anaglyph (red and blue lens) glasses distributed at all 7-11 locations. My folks and I gathered around the TV on a hot summer evening at 8 p.m. to tune in and watch the

much-anticipated event. I put the glasses on and stared for two hours.

If you remember this event then you probably remember being only mildly impressed. The broadcast quality was lukewarm at best, and I remember only a few parts of the movie actually translating into a 3D experience. The movie itself had a great storyline and was entertaining. But the 3D promotion was a huge let-down for me, as I was young, impressionable, and had my hopes built to the point that we'd have aquatic creatures floating around our living room. Even though the creature didn't reach out to try and strangle me that evening, it was still fun to stay up late and watch a horror movie as I sucked down a cola Slurpee®.

In just the last five years, I've noticed 3D making some serious leaps forward in availability and technology. It is being touted once again as the next video experience era, but this time the advocates are substantiated by real effects. I felt this section of the book should be written just to bring everyone up to speed on where we are, the technology that exists, and where we are headed with it as it relates to marketing.

There are two types of 3D technology that exist and are the most relevant to where we are headed - stereoscopy and auto-stereoscopy. Stereoscopy uses special liquid-crystal glasses that synchronize the lenses to shutter (open and close) opposite each other. When viewing video or animation that was composed with depth information (shadows, foregrounds, etc.), the lenses on the glasses only allow one eye or the other to view at a given microsecond. When one shutter is closed, the other is open. This happens around 60 times per second, which is too quick for your brain to detect any "shutter." The end result is two images at slightly different angles allowing your brain to decipher and fill in the depth, causing a very real image that appears in three dimensions.

Auto-stereoscopy doesn't require special glasses and will therefore be the *mother lode* as far as I am concerned. Consumers aren't going to go out of their way to wear special glasses 24/7 just to see 3D video when it's presented. Auto-stereoscopy will be the next-best thing to holograms once it is perfected. The potential opportunities are worth technology taking its time to bring auto-stereoscopy 3D to the masses. In the positions I've held with companies, I have been extremely fortunate to have witnessed several presentations utilizing this technology where it stands today.

Sales executives looking for me to buy this format brought to their presentations several monitors that had this technology built into the screen, along with specially produced animation and video. I watched as they revealed dozens of examples where one of our products could be inserted into a video and literally pop off the screen surface, giving me the illusion that I could reach out and grab it. This was the first time I had ever experienced this technology without the need for glasses, and it was quite impressive.

Unfortunately, there are still some drawbacks to auto-stereoscopy. For one, the effect can only be experienced when you are sitting dead center. Moving yourself too far to the left or right reduces the effect. In addition, there is a lot of time and preparation required to shoot video for this format. Even though the software helps incorporate depth information as the video is played, it won't be 100-percent impactful unless the original footage was shot using a number of cameras and angles. Hence, the costs are still in the stratosphere.

What strikes me as interesting is how quickly 3D is making its way to the masses. Even though special glasses are needed, we are already witnessing PC video game graphics cards evolving to include 3D experiences. As we move forward and the non-assisted 3D viewers become more and more affordable, it is likely that we will begin seeing video displays with 3D technology out in public. This is another example where the speed of information today significantly impacts the emergence of media technology to a great degree in the length of time between advancements.

Imagine your product or brand someday presented to the consumer in a multi-angle, truly 3D environment. How much impact would you have on someone who can see all angles of your product as if it was rotating inches from her face? I can remember *every* example of auto-stereoscopy that I witnessed during those presentations. And we all know how important brand recollection is. The next step in auto-stereoscopy availability will be a presence in storefronts, box offices or any other place where they can be viewed by the public. As the costs to produce this content dwindle, television and video monitor manufacturers will quickly glob on to make it available to the average consumer.

I'm convinced this *will happen* less than 10 years from now. I also fully expect that a re-emergence of television commercials and video presentations will occur utilizing this new format. Advertising professionals will flock to be able to offer their brands with more visual depth to the viewers with billions spent on production. There's nothing we can do today but wait. However, once this comes around full circle, be prepared for an uplifting and refreshing way in which we produce our commercials. We are very, VERY close.

Chapter X
Widgets, Gadgets and Interactive Apps

This is possibly the most fascinating form of emerging media with the most implication of marketing opportunity. Within literally a span of five years, widgets and applications ("apps") have become the hottest sector in marketing. Perhaps it's because this form of media implies much more than advertising, branding or even direct response. They incorporate the notion of loyalty and customer communication.

For those of you new to this area, think of these small packets of software as extensions of your Web site. The difference is they are portable, affordable, distributable, shareable and, most importantly, customizable for our marketing needs. There has been an explosion of service and development agencies offering to support your widget initiatives from development to distribution. The funny thing is that widgets and gadgets have actually been around for quite some time in the form of Java®. As media and communication and development software have progressed, the original Java-like program has grown legs and is now called an *app*.

First, let's define the three terms as they will be used in this chapter both synonymously and as separate expressions:

Widget: A software *element* that performs a specific function using a graphical interface manipulated by users to provide data important to them.

Gadget: A device or control that is used for a specific function. Usually found on a user's computer desktop.

Apps: Abbreviated term for *application*.

Widgets can be developed for a number of reasons and initiatives important to accomplish interactive marketing objectives. The costs are affordable, and we have at our disposal a number of channels for distribution thanks to their portability. In earlier years we were forced to purchase applications and software titles from retail stores in order to have a cool screen saver or word-processing solution. Today, not only can we simply download software to suit our needs, but in many cases we get it for free.

I'll take a step out on a limb for a moment to say the initial use (or should I say "misuse") of downloadable apps was what steered users away from adaptation for about six years. If it wasn't for this misuse, this emerging tactic would already be on its way to third or fourth generations of strategy. But, as it is, we are at the dawn of implementation.

Gator - now called Claria Corporation - was the first company to offer applications in the form of shareware. Formed in 1999, they offered free virtual wallets, music-sharing programs and other downloads with utility that could be quickly installed. From 1999 to 2004 more than 35 million PCs had installed some form of shareware on their computers. As many of us know, the free software didn't turn out to be exactly *free,* as many users found themselves the targets of uncontrollable pop-ups and unauthorized monitoring for marketing purposes. Most users never read the *fine print* found in the end-user license agreement (EULA) that alluded to this repercussion.

Once this was discovered, there was huge retribution for Gator and other companies engaging in these practices. It was contended that Gator took advantage of the fact that no one read the EULA, allowing them to force intrusive ad units into the user experience. Advertising more than paid for the cost for Gator to create this software, as a multitude of marketing professionals used them to target users searching for particular keywords as well as surfing sites that held content matching the marketer's product offerings.

The term "spyware" was coined and is now the distinguisher between user-accepted applications and downloads taking advantage of their behavior. Although Gator changed its name to Claria Corporation and made a stab at offering legitimate advertising based on user behavior, they still found themselves under the shadow of the past with every ad-blocking, anti-spyware application putting them at the top of the blacklist.

Take a few steps back and put your feelings about spyware aside for a moment. You will realize that the only difference between Gator products and acceptable widgets today is that they altered system registries to force advertising the user didn't want. Branded applications with utility are still the common thread in apps. Marketers have simply learned from the past and are more mindful of the user's preferences. A big part of emerging media and marketing tactics is adaptation from past mistakes.

Fortunately, the public is still open to obtaining free widgets and gadgets that serve a specific need. Otherwise, this area of marketing would still be a taboo and the opportunities to us as marketers would be lost. As you continue reading, this chapter will convey the effectiveness of feeds, why widgets and apps are such a useful form of communication, how they intertwine with social media, and the ease of their development.

The Truth About RSS

This is a perfect time to briefly discuss feeds. Perhaps you've heard buzz development terms such as XML or "RSS." They are the key ingredients to most shared applications, widgets, etc. In particular, RSS is dictated using the XML language and is the common linguistic used across all feed-based applications, accepted by the World Wide Web Consortium (W3C).

RSS stands for Really Simple Syndication. This format is typically used to publish content that is updated frequently. Common uses are news feeds, video publishing, blog entries, etc. Other tidbits such as date and authorship can be found in the accompanying metadata. The content is all fed through a standardized format so Web publishers can syndicate their work automatically. Users benefit because it allows them to aggregate content on the Web they want to review regularly in one place using an RSS reader or "feed" reader.

1999 was the year RSS became available, however its evolution into common use wasn't until 2005 with the commonly used icon seen on many Web pages and browsers. This latency in acceptance by Web users probably stems from the difficulty first experienced when setting up feeds for consumption. Any developer will tell you there's nothing "simple" about RSS. The simplicity is based on the ease of transference, not in development.

When RSS was first established, there weren't many options available for users to aggregate and experience content feeds the way they were meant to be. Early feed readers took a lot of time and patience to setup. Common Web users rejected this due to the cumbersome properties and didn't fully adopt RSS until five years later. Interesting to note most RSS feeds that were used took on a new form to the extent that ordinary users didn't realize it was RSS. They were widgets.

After all, which is easier? Finding your feeds, specifying their location in a feed reader, setting the retrieval intervals, and designating formatted parameters *or* simply "click here to install" or "grab-and-share"? Most Internet users would opt for the latter action. Almost all widgets and apps today with utility employ a feed for updates. But users don't care how they get the information; they just want to have a simple tool that pulls it in.

Goodbye Email, Hello Feeds!

The persistence of widgets and apps is such that they may be a vehicle to someday overtake email marketing. It makes perfect sense when you look at it from the viewpoint of Web 2.0. Our new generation of Internet and Web design commands the fostering of communication, information sharing and collaboration. Consider the following comparisons between feed-based software and email marketing:

Email is used for *promotion*
    ...Feeds *stream promotional* messages
Email is sent to *registered users*
    ...Feeds communicate with *anyone*
Email is read inside an *email client*
    ...Feeds can be read on *multiple platforms*
Email is *limited* by message size
    ...Feeds can download *any* file size
Email has to be *designed*
    ...Feeds are *pre-designed*
Email is *permission*-based
    ...Feeds have been pre-*permitted*
Email can be perceived as *SPAM*
    ...Feeds are *user-initiated*
Email communicates *a* message
    ...Feeds communicate message*s*

Email is *push marketing*
   ...Feeds are *pulled* by the user
Email is used with *ongoing cost*
   ...Feeds are used with *no cost*

See the advantages? Apps and widget communication make email look more and more cumbersome from every aspect. Email can be a tricky area to navigate as many have found while working through unfortified SPAM complaints, blacklist assurances, A/B split testing and copy optimization to enhance open rates.

A key area to take notice of is that email marketing is a "push" messaging tactic. Push messaging opens you up to a world of challenges where some users, even after opt-in, find your campaign to be intrusive or junk. Inevitably your email marketing will land in a SPAM filter or junk folder, which is typically nothing more than extra items for the user to delete in mass quantities without ever reading. One advantage I find to be of particular interest is that feeds are not "pushed" like email - they are "pulled" in by references within the software. This "pull" is a much different perspective than a user opting in to receive email messages. They have installed the widget, openly accepting updates when they are available.

In addition, the loyalty and click performance of users is five times better than an email subscriber. You may have less distribution of widgets and apps, but the quality of the user makes up for the difference; 100,000 email addresses might not even be close to the same quality as 20,000 app downloads or widget installs. Widgets are more than just a communication channel. To the user, they are valuable enough to take up real estate on his Web page or memory on her smartphone.

Best of all, the space has matured enough to where many of your standard email subscribers would warmly welcome the opportunity to download your widget. This presents a great scenario for marketers looking to migrate over to this new communication tactic. Once the development of your widget is complete, a simple announcement to your email subscribers is all that's needed to instantly have a networked channel.

Unfortunately, email marketing was ignored as a valuable resource until the economic downturn in late 2008. Companies everywhere decided to tap their email list resources and relentlessly, "beat the shit" out of their database in an effort to drive incremental revenue. Many companies I had subscribed to in the past, receiving only a few updates per year, were now sending multiple messages in a given month. The churn rate of email recipients has increased during this time, forcing marketers to find other forms of distributing their message or offer.

Design and Development

The word to keep in mind when your widget or app development begins is "utility." Building a communication device for the sole purpose of marketing and promoting your product won't be enough reason for users to keep it around. Instead of your primary focus on sales and revenue, you should be thinking of what your widget can offer that will provide a benefit to users. Promotional messaging and advertising should be built *around* the utility, not occupy the core of the utility itself.

Weather, news, games, instant messaging, calendars and even video diaries all have *utility* and could serve as a basis for the tool. Obviously, it is best to develop a tool relevant to your industry, unbiased and updated frequently. Just like virtual worlds, you need to contribute something to the audience at large to be adopted and accepted. Once you discover a reason for users to download and use your widget, the marketing and advertising implications will fall in place.

Start with an RFP to different creative studios and agencies for an idea or a design. The time to develop along with costs will vary depending on the format you wish to create. Widgets and gadgets for the Web can be created using common languages and software, taking less time and incurring reasonable costs. Creating an application or iPhone app with specific formatted parameters can take a little longer and bring your cost up significantly, depending on the intensity level of the features.

Logistics and Schematics

So what does it *actually* take to get started? Many companies love to initiate new tactics and strategies (such as social media) without understanding the true ramifications to overhead and resources. All apps and widgets work off of the same basic operations to update and communicate on a regular basis:

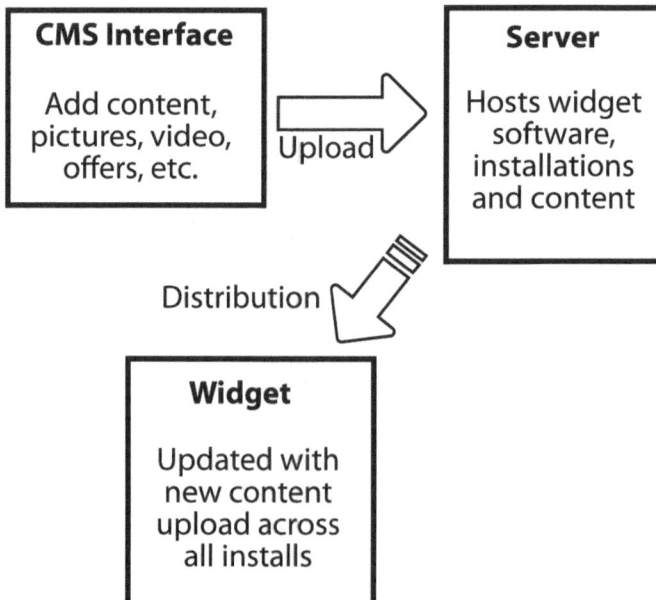

CMS Interface

Add content, pictures, video, offers, etc.

Upload

Server

Hosts widget software, installations and content

Distribution

Widget

Updated with new content upload across all installs

Widget content management is easily incorporated into your existing Web site content development and updating. Keeping in line with the thought that these are simply extensions of your Web site, it makes sense to keep the same process as you would for HTML content. The difference is that most widgets and apps have content management systems (CMS) inherent with the development itself. The CMS typically requires no programming language experience, so a marketing manager, coordinator or assistant can upload content whenever necessary.

This is an important aspect that implies the evolution of our interactive media today. The standard advertising process that we've become used to doesn't apply anymore. In the past we've had to endure a lengthy process to harvest leads and sales from the online audience. Create the online advertisement, build tracking links, create a landing page, optimize your Web site for conversions, etc. Fitting into the schematic of "halo media" (discussed toward the end of this book), widgets and desktop apps are communication platforms "anyone" can do with no programming experience. This is truly a look into our future, as online advertising has evolved to the point that it can be executed by any employee with no Web experience in a fraction of the time it takes for formal ad campaigns.

Building Your Network

Today there are a multitude of resources available for you to promote your application or widget. The most recommended (and affordable) way to distribute your tool is through existing resources. Remember that if you have a Web site, you've got traffic. If the traffic is significant, you already have a massive audience to distribute to. The same goes for your email marketing database of users who have opted-in for communication. Promoting to your existing audience will prove to be extremely beneficial when working within tight budgets. In addition, this gives you the opportunity to see how users react to your widget and how they use it. If your application or widget is viral enough, it may spread organically without much promotional effort behind it.

Social media channels are another cost-effective way for distribution. If you have a Facebook or MySpace presence that has built fans over time, this is an ideal place to start as well. In addition, most of these aggregated groups are going to be the biggest proponents of your company's product or services. They will serve as a perfect test-bed for your newly developed widget, openly offering more feedback than you will probably need. Fans are the greatest resource for spreading the word about anything your company communicates or produces. They will undoubtedly be an excellent resource of new-user widget acquisition.

If you are a newer company or don't have these audience resources at your disposal, you may need to put a small budget together to measure affinity. Always remember to test the waters before jumping in with a big-budget widget campaign. Even with a few thousand dollars, you should be able to draw an accurate conclusion of how useful the audience finds your tool once they copy or install.

There are a number of companies that have emerged as service providers when it comes to distribution. Some use the old-fashioned CPM method of advertising your tool's availability while others offer pay-per-install programs that may cost anywhere from 50 cents to $5 per acquisition. Depending on what your click rate and resulting ROI is, this may be an adequate equation for your venture to succeed.

One of the coolest things about your network is that it helps to identify valuable users *downstream* that adopt your tool into their sites and blogs. With proper tracking (usually available through your development agency), you can spot your most valuable widget users by how many second-generation downloads are happening. You may have 20 downloads and installs that go nowhere. However, there may be one or two in this group spawning off many downloads. This is where social media comes into play.

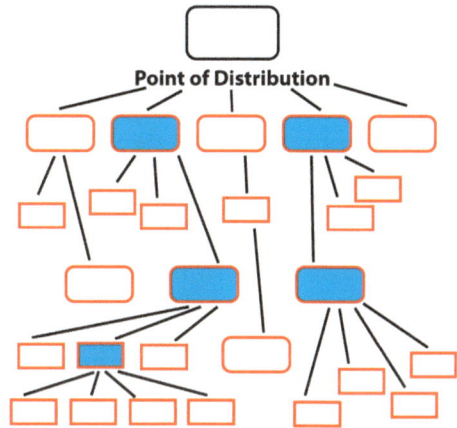

Point of Distribution

Historically, when encountering bloggers speaking highly of your company or claiming to be rabid fans, there was never a way to validate the number of users accessing their pages. Public aggregate reporting such as Alexa provided an index of assumed audience, but this has never been an exact science. The tracking mechanisms that can be used with widgets can provide additional insight into this area. Bloggers posting your widget for their audiences to see also provide a glimpse at how many users or impressions your widget receives. Coupling this with your social media efforts will identify your biggest influencers *out there* and give you a road map of contacts to reach out to and ensure a strong relationship with.

If the 20 downloads identify one user who has a subsequent second-generation download of 20 more individuals, you will undoubtedly want to make friends with this person for future communications. Widgets provide you the insight you need to accurately determine the key players engaged in social media. Aside from being an extension of your brand or promotional communications, this is one of the biggest benefits for developing tools that can be shared amongst the public at large.

In addition to updating your widget itself, the CMS can coexist with your Web site CMS. Many enterprise Web-based companies today already have CMS solutions in place. That being the case, there's no reason your Web site CMS can't also update your widget at the same time. Again, widgets and apps should be viewed as "extensions" of your Web site. If you truly take on this approach, you'll find an easy and efficient way to integrate the two.

A simple CMS for a widget allows URLs to be added as click-through links from the content to your site (or other landing pages). The URLs can be encoded just as you would for any click URL in advertising. Taking it a step further, the CMS can be developed with the intention of auto-encoding any URL added into the tool. Doing this would require an API interface with your advertising server but shouldn't be too much of a challenge as most ad serving companies are evolving to adopt this form of encoding as well.

This makes for a tool that is easily managed, updated and reported - leaving the main focus to be placed on distribution and building your audience.

EULAs

This book does not position itself to provide legal advice, as the author isn't versed, licensed or educated in legal matters. However, it is essential to note and understand the importance of end-user license agreements that protect your published widget or application. Always speak to your company's legal counsel to verify the applied use of your own EULA, which may have a variety of implications based on your industry, state, country or overall function. There aren't many marketers who *enjoy* going through this process, but because widgets and apps involve system incorporation, you would be well-served by getting the advice of an attorney on how the EULA should be written before turning your product loose within the public interactive realm.

The EULA is the contract between you and the users of your widget or application (which is also legally defined as "software"). It grants the user terms as to how they will use the software and where it will be applied. This agreement is critical because it outlines the basis for how the widget or application will be used and protects you in the following circumstances:

Usage: EULAs indicate the intention of how the application will be used. Desktop installations, copy to blogs and mobile installs can all be incorporated into the agreement that you convey to your users. Applying a utility in any other form creates an environment that could be subject to legal measures. This maintains your "ownership" of the tools and disallows modification by a hack or other means.

Copyright: EULAs also protect your copyrighted work as an individual or company. Therefore, any modifications of existing development can be deemed as a violation of these terms. In the world of "open source" and other non-restrictions, it is essential to claim your development to be used "as-is" with no post-production development allowed. That is, unless you are within an industry sector that thrives on crowd-sourcing the evolution of your product (such as Wikipedia). Proof of copyright can also be embedded within the code of your widget, making it easily identifiable should you find your application in use elsewhere. This is an age-old tactic developers have used for years where their comments or copyright notices are embedded within the programming, "commented out" to not impact the application's performance. Many developers hacking or infringing on copyrights are lazy and don't go through the code line by line, which keeps your copyright modification intact making it quickly identifiable when proof of copyright is needed.

Liability: Last but not least is the responsibility you are willing to accept (or not accept) with the end-user's acquisition and application of your "software." This is primarily important when your development is applied in the form of desktop or mobile downloads and installations. Any, and I repeat, *ANY* application downloaded and installed into an operating system *can* have adverse effects on performance. Although this is unlikely through the professional knowledge base of developers today, it simply takes into the consideration that individual personalization of end-user computer and mobile platform profiles can be unique to what is considered the common denominational norm of consumer electronics today. Although 99.99 percent of the time your application will be installed with no issues, there's that very small *chance* that a consumer's platform will react negatively to a system's registry addition. This is why your liability extensions should be clearly defined. The EULA will explain what impact your application will have (or not have) within the end-user's computer system and the associated risks the user may be taking when using your product. For the most part, this component of your EULA should alleviate you of any responsibility for any malfunction of equipment based on your downloaded application and subsequent installation.

Chapter XI

Getting Rich on
Rich Media

Getting "rich" on rich media can be interpreted by you in two ways - either *rich* by enhancing your bottom line in sales or *rich* by "enriching" your current online advertising creative. The truth is that rich media has evolved to where both perspectives apply.

I still remember the first animations I saw developed in Flash. It was a crudely made piece that played in a Web browser from JoeCartoon.com that featured three flies getting stoned. The first "page takeover" ad I saw was on AZCentral.com (the Web site for Phoenix-based *The Arizona Republic* newspaper) featured an online advertisement for a local car dealer. Cars sped across the page and jumped into an ad that was housed in the right rail of the page.

Adobe Flash made its appearance on the Internet scene in 1996 as some of you may recall first seeing with the publishing of Shockwave.com. Today, more than a decade later, it is used in a variety of applications from ad units to desktop downloads and has escalated the possibilities with regard to marketing application.

Perhaps some of you have already used Flash for animated design or Web site development. This section of the book is dedicated to identifying the uses of rich media using Flash as a foundational programming application and how it applies to our marketing needs. Professional developers have extreme know-how of how to make Flash perform certain tasks or serve specified purposes. It's up to us to identify the needs we have for rich media application and outsource the appropriate talent to design what we need it to do in the advertising space.

The appropriate definition of "rich media" is elusive. Rich media is nothing more than a concept used to describe applications that appeal to the various senses of sight, sound and interactivity. When someone refers to "rich media" as animation, she is correct. When someone refers to "rich media" as streaming music through an advertisement, he is correct. When someone calls an ad that expands as a result of a *"mouse over"* rich media, they are correct. There isn't one simple development software or language that embodies the concept of rich media. Rich media is simply the presence of the "application" appealing to our senses within specific online content. Throughout your marketing career you will run across many people who call Flash "rich media." In actuality, Java, AJAX or any other programming language can be considered rich media depending on how it is used.

The majority of what is deemed as rich media today *is* a result of Flash development. Just don't confuse Flash as *being* rich media. Rich media today allows us to do things that were never available to us in '90s. As interactive marketers, the goal is for us to understand what *is* possible and then apply it whenever the need arises. You don't have to be a Flash specialist or developer to employ these aspects. Simply *knowing* what is possible is good enough, as most of your rich media projects will probably be outsourced.

Ad Units Becoming Applications

At this moment in time, we can stop thinking of our only limitations being .gif or .jpg ad units when we purchase online media. If you are still tied to these resources, you are truly behind the curve. Flash development allows us to create rich media that can ultimately serve as an application. Gone are the days of point and click. Rich media today has helped our efforts evolve to so much more.

Most large ad-serving companies such as DoubleClick, PointRoll or Eyeblaster offer rich media advertising in their service arsenal for media buyers. Your developers are given the specifications for placement, including size, file weight and other restrictions. The Interactive Advertising Bureau (www.iab.net) provides creative development guidelines used for both rich media and standard online advertising assets.

For a few years, rich media simply allowed for the fast downloading of enhanced color pallets and animations inherent within ad units. Today, those ad units are expandable, explorable and completely interactive to the extent that they can almost be considered applications in themselves. Marketers have explored the boundaries of rich media and pushed the limits of interactivity yielding results that have evoked strong conversion rates, viral effects and consumer brand engagement.

Rich media has turned into an application in itself. In order to reap the full-fledged benefits of this area, it's best to think outside the confines of advertisements we've been used to in the past.

Ad Formats

To further standardize ad formats discussed in this section, we'll abide by the formats outlined by the IAB. Most well-known content publishing Web sites today - where your online ads will most likely be seen - refer to the IAB standards for ad serving. However you want to use site-on-site ads (advertisements served on your own site that direct users to other content) is up to you. But for the commercial placement of advertisements on *other* Web sites, it's important to have a common denomination of development standards.

There are a number of different online ad formats that seem to increase over time as new approaches are experimented with and applied by progressive publishers. The following formats describe what is in use today.

In-page Ad Units
These are the standard advertisements every Web surfer has come to know. "Banner" ads are what they are most commonly referred to as. Three basic sizes (horizontals, squares and verticals) are typically found on most major content publishers. These may be animated, dynamic or interactive but stay within their size specifications.

Specifications for all formats with regard to file size and dimensions are adhered to by most Web site publishers today. The chart below helps outline the most common sizes of in-page advertisements used, with additional information available at www.iab.net.

Universal Ad Package Specs	Recommended Maximum Initial Download Fileweight	Recommended Animation Length (Seconds)
300 x 250 IMU - (Medium Rectangle)	40k	:15
180 x 150 IMU - (Rectangle)	40k	:15
160 x 600 IMU - (Wide Skyscraper)	40k	:15
728 x 90 IMU - (Leaderboard)	40k	:15

Takeover
The takeover advertisement is becoming as common as a standard banner ad. As the user becomes inundated with the media, the takeover ad can be perceived as an annoyance as well as a meaningful message. Page takeovers can range from "peelbacks" to floating ads.

Video
More popular than ever is interlaced video within online ad units. Deemed as one of the biggest attention-getters, video can be imposed on almost any format and category of online advertising creative. If your ad employs video, it can mean a big difference with the interactivity you receive from the audience.

There are two types of video ads commonly used today: linear video advertisements and non-linear video advertisements.

Linear video ads occur with advertising in-stream, placing your message in a sequence of video presentation. The video typically takes advantage of a full window viewer, while the messaging is placed before, after or in between video segments. In many cases, the video plays first within an ad unit, inviting you, the user, to interact with the remainder of the advertisement.

Non-linear video ads are employed when the advertiser desires their message be present concurrent with the video playing. Graphic overlays or video embedded in a small area of a larger advertisement are examples of this approach.

The IAB has published specifications for both formats. Again, these parameters only serve as common denominators amongst most well-known publishers. You might find the need or opportunity for special treatments when dealing directly with the site on which you wish to advertise.

Expandable
Third-party ad servers such as Eyeblaster and PointRoll have been able to take ad units to a new level by offering platforms making them expandable, compelling and interactive. The expandable ad typically presents the user with a variety of unique features to explore a brand or a "special offer." They have served the advertiser well in lifting interactivity with the brand as well as capturing attention.

Expandable ads should be engaged through user-initiated input (mouseover), with the maximum width of the ad expanding to twice the initial size.

Floating Ads
This online advertising format appears to be "floating" over a page of content. A successful floating ad takes into consideration what is deemed as "non-intrusive." Best practices such as including a "close" or "skip" button are often implemented in order to accommodate user preferences. These are also commonly delivered through third-party ad servers. Floating ads themselves have become less common as very few implementations are found to be non-intrusive to the user.

Transitional Ads
Also known as "between-the-page" ads, these became popular around 2004 as more publishers found a way to monetize page transitions with users, thereby expanding their offerings. Transitional ads are usually allowed a run time of 10 seconds, unless engaged by the user. They also must be accompanied by "skip this ad" messaging, which offers users more control.

Dynamic Content and Other Components

RSS allows marketers to make instant changes to all ads in rotation (much like widgets). This greatly increases the efficiency of messaging and engagement in times that are appropriate for boosting sales. Price-sensitive commodities sold online such as airfare, tickets or hotel rooms can quickly change out starting rates without having to redevelop their ad units and resubmit for rotation.

Both content messaging and click-through redirection can be changed using a backend interface easily developed by your creative studio. The creative developers can assign the content parameters and set the area designated to pull in the message feed. Last-minute deals for holiday shoppers or getaway destinations are examples of practices for marketers taking advantage of dynamic content.

Another potential use of dynamic content can be messaging generated by your users. It is possible to engage your audience to the extent that their feedback and interaction can be updated on your advertisements. Chat strings, message boards, picture uploads and other user-generated content can be used to attract the attention and engagement you're looking for. The more creative you are in integrating social-media aspects into advertising, the more likely you are to have a living, breathing advertising campaign that truly communicates in two directions.

Other components can be incorporated as well and are considered standard tactics when employing rich media applications. Ad units can be developed to pull in certain "dates of availability" or promotions as well as allow the user total control to query and explore different product characteristics without leaving the advertisement. This is where an advertisement may actually be considered a "tool" or utility for users as they discover different functionalities as means to an end.

Along with data pulls, rich media also affords the capability to obtain email address opt-ins and mobile subscriptions. I think this tactic is extremely underutilized, because most of us are looking for the quick click and purchase. Everything we implement should include some form of user data acquisition, allowing us to contact interested consumers later on through other channels. Backing your total revenue from email campaigns and SMS into your total subscriber base will give you an assigned "value" for each acquisition. This can also be used to evaluate the success of your rich media initiatives.

Rich Media Metrics

Through the use of online ad units we've become used to three primary metrics: Click-through rate (CTR), conversion rate and cost per conversion (or expense/revenue). Utilizing rich media, you will quickly find a few more metrics that are of interest:

Interaction Rate (IR) – This is the number of your rich media interactive impressions divided by rich media impressions. If your rich media advertisement was served 10 times and, out of those instances, two of those impressions experienced interaction, your IR is 20 percent.

Display Time – This is the average number of seconds your rich media ad is displayed to a user. A time "cap" is usually implemented after a couple of minutes to prevent skewing results due to users leaving their browsers open for long periods of time.

Expansions – This is the number of times a rich media ad unit was expanded and the duration of the expansion.

Expanding Time – The average time an ad was viewed in its expanded state.

Interaction Time/Rollover Rate – When a user clicks or rolls over a rich media ad, the total time is calculated in seconds to determine interaction time. Rollover rate by itself is determined by the number of times a user places his cursor over the ad divided by the number of ads served.

Video View Rate – This is simply the percentage of video viewed. If a user watches a :30 video for only 15 seconds, the view rate would be 50 percent.

Rich media metrics have not only provided additional insight to Internet marketers and media buyers, but they've also attracted the attention of another group. Offline media and branding experts especially pay attention to these metrics because they allude to the exposure of users to their company name or products. Although these metrics don't translate to hard-core conversion rates, they offer a measurement not found in any other media: brand exposure. This is another area where online tactics and offline traditional media measurement cross over.

Finally, rich media can incorporate recognized cookies on users' browsers in order to serve content within that is exclusive to them. For instance, if the user has visited Web sites that he's registered on, using his address or location, dynamic rich media ads can incorporate this into their messaging and say such things as, "Cold weather in Chicago? It's warmer in the Bahamas!"

This transcends across privacy concerns and should be used with caution. However, as users today mature in their interactive engagement, there is a better understanding of what personal identifiable information (PII) is and the level of acceptance. It's realistic to predict that rich media or other ad units will someday have the capability to speak directly to you. Imagine ad units being served using your name or phonetically speaking it aloud, telling you it's time to take a trip to Nassau. Today, this would freak people out a bit as there is still privacy sensitivity. Over time, users will eventually relinquish privacy most likely in the form of "user preference settings."

Chapter XII

Data Assessment in the Emerging Space

In the last chapter we discussed rich media metrics and acronyms associated with user engagement. This chapter will open the world up to the rest of the Web and interactive media covering metrics and tactical analysis relevant to emerging media today.

Old-school online media brought us two advertising disciplines: banner ads and search. The term "banner ads" makes me cringe today, because it evokes the thought of archaic practices used by webmasters "back in the day." Search advertising has remained consistent, although with the maturity of our online audience we may find some adjustments needed to keep it effective.

The mentality of online marketers' assessment of the transaction or acquisition process has been extremely linear in the past. The thought process behind any campaign (whether it was ROI- or branding-focused) was the basic "click-and-buy" perspective. With our entry into the digital age, this way of thinking has become merely a component of the whole.

Today's interactive media pushes content formats that aren't centered on your interactive presence (most likely your Web site). In fact, consumer discussions, research and purchase decisions are being made without your direct involvement at all. Without consulting your Web site, the response of your consumers when interacting with your brand or purchasing your product is evident at *arm's length* from your primary online presence. These interactions are discussed in the next chapter, "Halo Media", as you read on to see what cornerstones are essential to be in front of your users at the most critical time.

For now, let's examine the metrics used to assess and analyze user behavior within the emerging media environment. Everyone uses metrics for different reasons, whether it's branding, purchase processes, conversion metrics, or purchase windows. Tracking your users is the key to proving *or disproving* specific strategies and becomes even *more* critical when entering the emerging media space.

Some of the strategies and perspectives of these metrics correlated with certain goals are based on the opinion of the author, not fact. Each and every industry engaged with new media tactics should base their evaluations on what is important to them. In some cases it will be audience reach or interactivity. In other instances it will be solely based on the company's bottom line. Whatever situation you find yourself in, always resort to your overall goals and what tracking is needed to provide an accurate assessment and recommendation to your company.

Assessing Your "Cookies"

In the past, Internet marketers were granular. They focused all their attention on impressions, clicks, traffic and subsequent revenue. Emerging media today demands we look at this tracking perspective merely as a component of the whole. Stimulating future sales is just as important as the online sales process itself. It used to be completely acceptable to find a Web site with users who match your ideal audience, place advertising units, and observe the resulting traffic. Not anymore.

Users themselves have matured in the way they use the Web. The last big jump in online users entering the Web was around 2001–2003. Today, most users have almost a decade of experience and maturity behind them in how they are using the Internet and interactive mediums to manage their daily lives. Simply put, our online audience has "evolved" in their way of thinking and pattern of behavior. In some situations, display ads are becoming more and more ignored by the user who is seeking a more contextual encounter with your brand through research or social media–based conversation.

This should not imply that your Internet advertising creative should be trashed with a pure focus on contextually relevant strategies. It simply means that user attention has expanded to include time spent or allocated on other mechanisms.

Unfortunately, moving away from exclusively observing linear tracking leads us to another "fuzzy" area that is sometimes more speculative than factual. I recollect arguments with brand professionals during my early years with regard to the importance of penetration and frequency when purely seeking direct return. Now it seems that some of those branding arguments are holding a bigger stake in your overall conclusion.

The best place to start is where most Internet marketing specialists get their information about traffic and conversions: the cookie. Cookies have been around as long as there have been Web analytics and have remained the primary source of data most of us use to make our optimization recommendations and overall assessments. Without cookies, we would completely be in the dark about what is happening. Cookies have had their share of faults and general integrity attacks but have remained as the number-one source of user information. Alternatives to-date have not proven to be reliable or feasible as they have failed to provide the same data as cookies while alleviating privacy concerns by users.

With regard to acquisition (or revenue) metrics, there are two primary "types" of cookies used today: the *view* cookie and the *click* cookie.

> *View* cookies are served and recorded on a user's browser when an ad is served (not to be confused with when an ad is "seen"). So long as an advertisement is loaded onto a page, whether on the top or at the bottom, the cookie is loaded, remaining on the user's browser cache.

> *Click* cookies for the most part "trump" view cookies. These usually replace the view cookies after a user clicks or engages with your advertising.

"Viewable" area of page

"Unseen" area of page

Ad unit served, with cookie retained on browser

The ongoing debate is around the expiration of cookies. When is the appropriate time to expire your view cookie? Or your click cookie? Is it fair to measure and take credit for a view cookie (where the users either did or *did not* see your advertisement) that doesn't expire for 90 days? Did that advertisement *really* influence the purchase behavior months after it was first recorded? Should your *click* cookie get credit for a sale? Or had the user been served multiple *view* cookies beforehand, therefore influencing their behavior for sure?

Believe it or not, this debate is more monumental than one may think. There are many, *many* companies and agencies that use an extended expiration on the view cookies and inappropriately record and take credit for revenue that simply isn't valid. You can imagine the down-line impact as the client or company sees the results and says, "Holy shit! We only spent $50,000 and tracked over $10,000,000 as a result? Don't bother asking me *if* I want to spend more money! Where do I sign?"

But who is to say what an appropriate duration for the cookie is? Even if a company is in the same industry as another, both will use different expiration dates. Some companies will have their *view* cookie expire in a few days, with their *click* cookie lasting a lot longer. Some will have both types of cookies expiring at the same time. It's somewhat concerning that there is such a vast discrepancy across companies within the same business. If advertising spending is based on false pretenses (assuming the user had seen an advertisement when they really didn't), then there's a lot of money going to waste that does nothing more than make the internal Internet marketing department or advertising agency "look good."

There certainly needs to be some consistency across businesses using *click* and *view* cookies to determine and measure advertising effectiveness. To my surprise, the SEC hasn't yet gotten involved with this area which, indeed, they should. The only guidance I can offer is to observe your purchase cycle. Are the majority of your product purchases made fairly quickly by consumers? Or is the purchase cycle a little more lengthy, often finding the user taking considerable time to research and seek advice before making their purchase decision? Books, movie tickets and music are rather instantaneous decisions, while cars, houses and cruises may take most of us longer to decide.

A user looking for a car may be influenced by *multiple* ad units the manufacturer is placing. When the conversion is tracked by user inquiries (submitted forms), the auto dealer or manufacturer will probably value the *view* cookie a lot more since the acquisition isn't actually revenue, it's just one step closer to the purchase process; whereas a cruise line would place a lukewarm value on the *view* cookie, attributing almost all their success to *click* cookie reporting.

My opinion is to use the *click* cookie–measured revenue as the end-all in assessing your ad performance. *View* cookie revenue is a good measurement to indicate you are advertising in the right place at the right time for potential sales but shouldn't be as highly regarded as the *click*. The *click* is undeniable; the *view* is subjective.

Leaving this "absolute" perspective behind us for a moment, let's take a look at where the value of a *view* cookie really fits into the equation. What if one were to allow the *view* cookie to be extended for a year or more? Would there be a concentration of users purchasing at different times? Perhaps we would see many conversions happening through our *click* cookies around the holidays, which may be contributing to the *view* cookie stored on browsers that have loaded our advertisement in the past. This may not justify the expense to advertise during the month of placement, but over the course of a year those placements may be more valuable, depending on how you look at your consumer's purchase-decision cycle.

In my mind, *click* cookie revenue and *view* cookie revenue should be assessed side by side. In other words, reporting the revenue from users who *clicked* and purchased against the number of *those same* users who also had a *view* cookie stored on their browser. This would indicate the level of influence our advertisements had on the user's purchase behavior. Afterward, we would take the remaining *view* cookies and place a lower value on their reported revenue contribution, as we still don't *know* that the users actually saw our corresponding advertisements.

Even if your advertisement is placed at the tip-top of a Web page, you don't know for certain it was *seen*. Therefore, *view* revenue should remain subjective and always be used with care in making future spending decisions.

What's *REALLY* Happening Here?

Beware of metrics. We all tend to eat, sleep, live and die by them, but they are NOT foolproof. As much as we all want some consistency in an inconsistent world of interactive media, relying on numbers that measure user behavior can be detrimental in your decision-making if they are wrong or interpreted incorrectly.

The main point I want to drive home is that not everything is always as it seems. If you notice a tactic performing badly, chances are you would go through the regular routine of double-checking the placement, the message and everything else you can think of before you ultimately pull it offline. The same goes for something performing well; you double-check everything before making the decision to spend more time and money on it.

I have seen several instances of the surface reporting actually providing an inaccurate view of what was really happening. Hopefully, through these examples, everyone will understand how important it is to *dig deeper, ask questions,* and *put together a comprehensive view* of the situation.

Degradation of Ad Unit Performance
Over the past couple of years, I've noticed a big change (for the worse) in display advertising performance. In the

case of rich media ads, the regular interaction rates were there and normal view times with video were present. The drop-off was with the actual revenue. My online media buyers assured me they had checked and re-checked their negotiated placements, had seen the ads in rotation and tested all the clicks and corresponding reporting. Yet the same revenue as before wasn't there. Comparing the number of clicks we'd seen from similar advertising creative and publishers in the past were the same. Same number of impressions, roughly the same click-through rates, etc. Yet the same revenue as before wasn't there.

I found it difficult to yank these placements and continuously divert our advertising away from publishers I *knew* had the right audience seeking our services. But at the same time, I couldn't deny what was being reported and had no basis as to why this was happening.
Until 2 a.m. on a Saturday morning.

Being the geek-partier-gone-family-man, I found myself writing some white papers late on a Friday night, turning into Saturday morning, while the kids and wife had long since gone to bed. I was doing some research and saw an advertisement on Yahoo! for a new Xbox game scheduled for release within a few days. Rarely do I click on an ad unit. But this time it was compelling enough to check it out, and my passion for gaming got the best of me .... And that's when it happened.

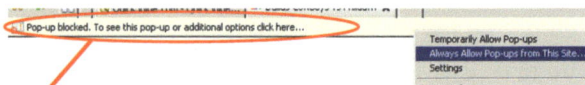

Pop-up blockers on popular web browsers prevent users from clicking through to your site. Once "allowed" in this environment, the page refreshes and your ad unit is lost in rotation with the user eventually moving on.

The pop-up blocker was set to block both automatic and user-initiated separate windows. I forgot to use the "Ctrl" key override, so when the click was initiated, I saw the standard message bar notice appear at the top of my Explorer 7 browser. It said "Pop-up blocked. To see this pop-up or additional options click here." The "options" were simple: Temporarily Allow Pop-ups or Always Allow Pop-ups From this Site. I selected to "Temporarily Allow Pop-ups". The screen refreshed and the ad unit was gone. After refreshing the page almost a dozen times, I never saw the ad again and decided to move on.

It occurred to me that this could be the reason for the decline of Internet ad unit revenue. Taking the following things into consideration:

- MS Internet Explorer has the most penetration of any Web browser in use today

- Over 81 percent of Americans use some sort of pop-up blocker with their browser (*New Scientist*, 2006, Issue 2582) – most likely even more today

- Most individuals set their pop-up blocker to "moderate" or higher; newer versions of Explorer have default settings

Until 2006, publishers generally allowed advertising clicks to load the advertiser's site within the same window. User time spent on-site is a retention metric publishers use to assign a value to their traffic. It would make sense, then, for them to pop up a separate window for advertisers instead of the transition to the new site happening in the same window. This keeps their users on their site longer and increases the time spent per user.

Now that separate windows are popped when ads are clicked, the pop-up blockers are working overtime. Subsequently, unless users perform an override such as holding the Ctrl key down, the page will refresh to allow the new pop-up allowance and the ad *disappears* into rotation. As impatient as Web surfers can be, there's not a chance on this green earth they will spend time refreshing the page to get their original ad served.

This certainly seemed like an answer to our problems with revenue we were used to seeing. The only workaround I've used ever since was to be sure to include as much content as possible when using a rich-media ad - something compelling enough to get users to visit your site in the event the ad disappears when they try to click through. This is actually a bigger issue for more Internet marketers out there and is a growing concern for achieving ad performance we all look for from our publishers.

Does Anyone "Get" the Bluetooth?

Another example I encountered with regard to metrics that don't reveal reasons for poor performance was when we first started using proximity marketing tactics. Previously we discussed expectations for user populations who have their Bluetooth devices turned "on." Those expectations were derived from past experience that had required a deeper look into the situation at hand.

Proximity marketing using Bluetooth was still an unknown for how it would work for my company at the time. We had done several tests with higher expectations than we should have had. The industry reported that approximately 35 percent of our audience *should* have their Bluetooth on, so we expected a certain number to receive messaging, potentially opting in. Unfortunately, we consistently saw a low number of users responding, but the data conveyed that our device was detecting a much higher number of Bluetooth-enabled devices.

Enabled, as it were, doesn't mean *turned on.* Looking into this further, we decided to place some signs indicating pedestrians were walking into a *Blue Zone,* after which we noticed a bump in accepted messages and were within the range of expectation. During our research, there was simply no one out there who explained how using signage could help instigate users to turn on their capabilities to receive promotional messages broadcasted.

Today, it's still important to focus on where the masses are, which is easier then worrying about signage. But it's interesting how a little additional "push" can really turn around your numbers.

Traditional Influences on Search

Making an on-the-spot decision can lead to disaster if you're wrong. It sounds like a "duh," but I think any Internet marketer can vouch for witnessing people who get excited yet still don't see the whole picture. This is usually encountered when clients or upper management see how much money they are making off of your efforts.

Search marketing has been, is and will be for some time to come the foundation and core ROI of any online media campaign. Although users are making their purchase decisions using references other than search, it still drives the most *trackable* revenue over any other source out there.

I've seen astonishing ROI in search as SEM has become a huge industry sector for online marketers and companies that specialize in paid search optimization. It appears that paid search is sometimes only limited by the number of dollars you throw at it. It's no surprise that companies have migrated budgets from other areas in order to fortify their SEM budgets.

The extreme decision is to make the choice in pulling all of your other advertising except for search. After all, you're making the most money from search so why not dump your entire budget into it, right? Wrong.

I'll tell anyone today, this is shortsighted thinking. It's true that "search" is a key ingredient for trackable revenue with a good ROI, but take another step forward and understand the reasons why:

1) Because everyone uses search engines to find companies and products/services

2) Because once optimized, your placements will appear at "the top"

3) Because search engines offer placements within contextual content on other sites

4) Because people *are already looking for your brand*

It's the fourth reason that begs to be researched a bit further. Why would customers *already be looking for your brand?* They've obviously already done their research or were prompted by advertising. Online advertising fuels search to an extent but not as much as I believe offline advertising does. When driving past a billboard or listening to a radio station, are you really going to dial the number on your cell phone? I'd be willing to bet that a very, VERY small percentage of people do that these days. They are more versed and mature in how to use the Internet and know they can *look up* any company they hear about.

Therefore, pulling back on your offline media is like throwing out the baby with the bathwater. Search is your biggest component of online revenue - why take away the components that fuel it?

The more you invest yourself in media - whether it is offline, online, mobile, social or any other emerging tactic - the more important it will be to ensure your SEM strategy is in place. It is important to understand it's not just your placement within a search engine making you money; it is also the offline media that encompasses your brand. It is the offline media that encompasses your target audience. It is that offline media impact that is sometimes "intangible."

Chapter XIII
Halo Media

In November 2008 I served as a keynote speaker at the PubCon conference at the Las Vegas Convention Center, and in front of 2,000 people I introduced the concept of "Halo Media." This is something that has surrounded us for quite some time but has become more and more apparent as we look at breakthrough tactics and emerging media. The attendees talked it up, and there were a few other speakers who picked up the buzzword.

Every interactive marketing communication outlet we use, every angle we take to garner audience and every new media channel introduced seems to take us further away from the "click-purchase" mentality. Web traffic isn't streamlined anymore. You can't just place a few ad units or search text and judge your successes by the clicks that come in as a result. Consumers are using the Web differently. Instead of click-buy, it's more like discuss-consult-compare-research-click-evaluate-buy.

Why is this more so today than in prior years? Again, it goes back to the maturity of most Web users and how they use the tools to manage their daily lives. Community doesn't only exist anymore within big publishers such as AOL or Yahoo!. There are tools abundant in all corners of the interactive space that allow users to connect and form their own communities without walls. Sites such as Facebook, MySpace, Twitter, Digg, and YouTube only serve as portals to a larger community that floats in, out and around all media online and emerging media offline.

Halo media attempts to describe and outline where the community groups are, where discussions are found, and specifically describe the media they are using. We are living in a time where new media and tools to reach people are popping up literally overnight. This is just the tip of the iceberg as we look toward the future. In order to define and quantify emerging media, it's best to paint a picture that explains where you and your business efforts stand in relation to it all.

Before moving further I'd like to re-emphasize that not all marketing channels are going to make sense for you and your business. The best thing to do is test on a smaller scale and see if it makes a significant positive impact on your bottom line. I say *significant* because there's no reason to stick with a particular channel or tactic if it's not doing much for you. There are plenty of other outlets to behold!

Once you have a comprehensive strategy for marketing communications, you will start to define your own Halo media plan and begin reaping the benefits through cross-channel consolidation. The beauty of the Halo is that your potential customers and target audience are most likely using the same channels. After diving into it further, you'll find out the different segments of commonality and can exploit them, creating frequency through *multiple* interactive mediums.

The goal of presence within your Halo is to be there at the right place at the right time. Fortunately, interactive media allows us to do this without a massive expense so long as it is done methodically and with appropriate measures. You want to be there when your potential customer has made her decision while *acting as a catalyst* during her purchase process. Perhaps it is a "teaser" message or even introducing a viral element that stimulates conversation. No matter what the message is, the goal is to make it easy for your consumer to find you and act on their decision to purchase your product.

This is the point where I am telling you that your interactive media should not all be qualified by the revenue brought in. Too often are the best interactive marketers in the world caught up in direct revenue. Direct-response revenue ignores all the other touchpoints with the consumer that may have happened during the purchase-decision process. You may continue to measure the revenue off of one particular channel all you want; just understand that one particular channel isn't the only source. It's only a tool.

As emerging media channels continue to introduce themselves, the astute marketer has to take into consideration that the source of revenue, whether it's a search placement or online advertisement, only serves as a tool for the user to find you. The chances of them seeing or "hearing" about your brand, product or service from other sources has significantly increased over time.

Years ago, I would have argued against this, taking nothing else into consideration other than one particular placement driving my business. But, unfortunately, the answers aren't that simple anymore. As media has evolved so must our perspective on identifying and measuring our consumer traffic resources. I've researched that as high as 70 percent of your customers attributing to a particular advertising placement have heard of your company or services from other sources prior.

So, back to Halo media and my attempt to paint an appropriate picture of what's happening. The *ring of audience* is divided into three specific segments that categorize the interaction: online media, offline media and emerging media. For now let's just say that "emerging media" is defined as anything interactive but not confined to the Internet. Here's how the Halo categories look:

Online	Emerging	Offline
Mini Sites	Social Media	Viral / WOM
Search	Mobile	Radio
Widgets	In-Game	Outdoor
Virtual Worlds	Video	Print
Video	Widgets	Video
Ad Units		

Web Site

Lots of outlets and lots of opportunity for audience. The key ingredient in your interactive marketing strategy and planning should be to secure a presence in each of the three sectors. Like it or not, you will need to produce video. EVERYONE responds to visuals, and while offline marketing specialists always deem television to be the most effective, I would argue that they actually mean "video" elements, not necessarily the medium.

Unless you have massive budgets and resources to manage your engagement in all areas, I would suggest securing at least *two* channels in each to ensure your presence. The wide net you are casting to encompass all of these tactics will cost tons of dollars and tons of man hours. Let's face it; most of us don't have access to unlimited resources to do this.

A secured, limited presence should garner the audience you are looking for as well as meet the goals for your brand identity and penetration. Remember, you are just looking to serve as a touchpoint. Think of it as putting a virtual portal to your company, products and services on the busiest street corners in a big city. Hopefully someday we'll be able to do that in the real world!

The "Long Tail" fits into this concept perfectly. New marketing techniques channel messaging to audiences using them which may not be considered the "masses" but can collectively make up a good portion of your potential consumers. This is especially true in the emerging media sector. By penetrating the Long Tail media areas, you will find that the 20 percent of the audience you gain can make up 80 percent of new marketing channel sales. Remember the Pareto Principle, also known as the 80-20 rule.

Chris Anderson of *Wired* magazine put it best when he said that the "future of media is already here, it's just unevenly distributed." Unfortunately, we as marketers and advertisers don't have the luxury of targeting the largest audiences through one media channel. Consumers have become much more diversified as they have decided when, where and how they are going to digest their media. Because of this we are forced to seek them out and discover where our most relevant, qualified consumers are in terms of how they use media technology today.

For some companies this may include iPhone applications. For others it may mean advertising in virtual worlds. As we move into this new era of fragmented media, it's always going to be important to test, retest and test again everything that comes across our desks in terms of opportunities. The more cheaply you can test, the better off you are. But be sure to test everything you can because the one you miss out on may be the one that strikes gold for customer acquisition.

I wish I could tell everyone that all we need to do is focus on several mediums, but that's simply not the case. It will *never* be the case. Our channels have been splashed across the entire world with more being developed every day, and there's nothing we can do about it. The sooner marketers both young and old alike agree that they have to be proactive the sooner new media will be assessed properly with the cream rising to the top. It's not an easy situation, as all companies look for ROI in terms of direct sales.

Whether or not you can track direct response will depend on the particular channel you decide to test. Some will be easier than others, but the Halo Media concept looks at all corners around your company and proclaims success based on overall marketing revenues, not attributed to one source.

Chapter XIV

So What About "The Cloud"?

One of the most fascinating and "geekiest" topics you can research today is the evolution of "cloud computing." It describes a world we're headed toward with regard to data storage, accessibility and technology in communications. The cloud positions interactive media in a space that occupies no physical resources and allows us engagement anywhere and anytime. Cloud computing was first introduced in concept in 1960 by John McCarthy, awarded for his contributions to artificial intelligence. He claimed that "computation may someday be organized as public utility." We can discuss the future all we want, but this is the most accurate statement with decades of projection I've seen.

Cloud computing harnesses all resources across the Web while providing access to software and services on an as-needed basis. With all the data available today, multiple resources are required to store, manage, analyze and process critical items we need on a daily basis. We've all seen instances of cloud

computing in the past (SETI@home, Salesforce.com) but weren't really consciously aware of it until recently.

This concept will allow us more freedom than we have ever realized. It will introduce the elimination of physical space necessities as well as the conveniences we've been seeking for quite some time. No cables, no computer towers at our feet, and no need for large retail categories. As humans in the digital age, we've evolved beyond the need for many things physical.

A World *Without* Cables

Although wireless technology doesn't have a lot to do with cloud computing, it will make the access to it seamless. As we move closer to a "cloud state," access will be key and the public will eventually recognize WiFi as a free resource to communicate.

Some WiFi areas are free, others are not. The theory is that as wireless broadband and connectivity become more and more frequently established and used, the paid hotspots will dissolve. So, to all you hotels out there that charge me almost $20 for wireless connections ... get ready to make it free!

There's much more money to be gained by services the cloud will offer than there is through wireless subscription fees. Just recently, airlines introduced WiFi access during travel. Eventually, we'll be able to have access everywhere, in the most remote areas. There's simply too much commerce to be carried out for this not to happen.

First attempts to make city-wide WiFi access available proved to be more difficult than originally thought. In 2005, Sunnyvale, California, was the first metro-based area to offer WiFi access to its citizens. Few additional cities were successful, with the majority of others put on hold. As the years have gone by, components have been developed to be faster, cheaper and more easily installed. We can all expect our hometowns to offer this access within the next decade or so.

A World *Without* Retail

Perhaps the largest *noticeable* impact the cloud will have in the physical realm is the absence of retail items. Anything that can be digitized will be and therefore won't be necessary to be present on physical formats. Music stores, video stores, electronic boutiques and photo marts will all be unnecessary. These consumer goods alone make up about half of the retail space in shopping malls and plazas, so it will be interesting indeed to see the void where they once were. More importantly, *what* will take their place?

Is it really so hard to imagine? Children today will never know or understand digital formats on physical hardware. Everything we need will be at the click of a button for the cheapest price. I remember spending a lot of time in the '90s battling online users any way I could to make sure they felt I was a "safe" online merchant. Third-party services such as VeriSign® played a huge role in customer assurance. Now that most consumers feel comfortable buying products and services online, the battle is over.

Users will feel completely confident in their purchase and downloading of media. Whether it be movies, albums or software, major companies have made huge strides in this area in order to push this activity mainstream. We are literally a few steps away from having everything available within the cloud. Of course, there will always be those who *need* something *physical* to feel "good" about their purchase. I would venture to say that folks will end up paying a premium to have merchandise mailed to them that could otherwise be digital. The physical presence of digital media has already reached a comfort level for many consumers by the way of flash drives, MP3 players or other forms of compact recording devices.

A friend of mine pointed out that the real estate collapse of 2008/2009 will force retailers to focus even more on "e-tailing." For years, mainstream storefronts have been comfortable investing in their physical locations, with new branches and satellite stores everywhere. With overhead costs reaching astronomic proportions when it comes to retail, these companies are in the middle of taking a heavier look at their opportunities online. In the past, they've been comfortable with their online sales and presence as an afterthought, allowing online affiliates to take a good chunk of their proceeds.

Comparing the cost of digital media between physical CDs, DVDs, and other formats against the cost of electronic storage, waiting for downloads is a no-brainer. As new and younger marketing generations grow older and attain more spendable income, they will already be used to the cloud and working their way to consumer satisfaction through digital digestion.

In the past we observed that Kazaa and Napster provided free services that allowed peer-to-peer sharing of digital media. We also observed their fate as pirated copies of albums, movies and software were transferred from one user to another seamlessly. Although this was illegal, it was a realistic look into our future in terms of the ease of availability. Digital rights management (DRM) continues to make a play (no pun intended) to maintain the integrity of intellectual property, ensuring consumers get what they pay for. However, the workarounds for re-recording media layered with DRM are numerous and even outlined in Wikipedia. The freedom of information will eventually overcome DRM technology, and we will see a new age of file sharing and implementation such as Bit Torrent.

The cloud works around the concept of users only paying for the resources they use. Whether this is positioned as a public utility or company-specific logins, the money will be undoubtedly harvested from us, guaranteed.

A World *Without* Physical Storage

Yes, I'm looking forward to the day I don't need to have a computer housing unit under my desk constantly blocking my feet from a good stretching. Storage in the cloud will be achieved on major server farms and peer-to-peer contributions performing collective processes. Increased high-speed bandwidth and connectivity allows for the same response times as if users were tapping a centralized processing infrastructure.

A World *With* Behavioral Monitoring

My definition (and probably your definition) of privacy today will be different from consumers of the future. The cloud encompasses more than just computing activity. Eventually all media such as TV, radio, VOIP, SMS, gaming and Internet browsing will be tied together. Microsoft has already pioneered steps in this direction as they originally took massive losses on their Xbox and Xbox 360 products. The goal was never to make a profit with the release of their gaming system. Their vision was projected *decades* down the road, as the end game is to own a piece of real estate in the majority of households. With more than 28 million units sold worldwide by 2009, they are well on their way.

If you think the cloud only has implication with PCs or laptops, guess again. The services and storage characteristics available reach beyond your computer. Resources will be available to any device that *connects to it*. DVRs, streaming radio, etc., are all devices that will one day be in communication with the cloud. It stands to reason that behavioral targeting will take on a whole new level that none of us can fathom at this moment.

I'll take a stab at describing what I see as a futuristic expectation. Within the environment where all media is tied together, our activities as consumers can be easily monitored and interpreted in order to engage us at the right time with the right message. Text messages, interactive commercials we respond to, and videos downloaded to a myriad devices are just a few behavior patterns that will be of interest to next-gen marketers.

I'll even venture to suggest that our computers (or interfaces) will know ahead of time what we are looking for and provide "recommendations" (rather than results) for us to review by the time we sit down to do serious shopping. This will be seen as a convenience for most people out there, as it will eliminate the need to search their own resources. Social consulting and referral will still be a mainstream form of research before purchase, but it will be more difficult to separate organic peers from an extension of "paid" advocates.

By now some of you are saying, "What about privacy? Many consumers would never give up their right to be protected against that level of tracking!" And you're right; many wouldn't, in the way of your thinking *today*. Do we really think that privacy issues today will concern the consumers (our children) of tomorrow? In the future, *privacy* will be given up in the form of *preferences*. "Would you like more information including special offers about cruises to Mexico?" the TV will ask. "Yes" is what many consumers will answer. In an environment with all media tied together, tucked away somewhere in the user agreements will be the stipulation that allows your future activities and reviews on travel content to be tracked, which will subsequently supply you with your interest needs within other media.

Prompts such as, "Would you like recommendations for products you are researching on your TV or computer?" will be answered with a quick "Yes," and then we'll find our daily lives supplemented with opportunities around what we are currently researching to buy. Today, behavioral targeting is pretty much limited to our Web surfing habits. Taking it over the horizon will open it up to all media where "recommendations" can be made.

It makes sense to ease our lives by setting our preferences for when, where and what media messaging will be delivered to us. The perception will be, of course, that we will benefit by saving time with the luxury of offers finding us, rather than us looking for offers. But in the meantime, pieces of our private information will be given up in exchange for these desires.

A World *Without* "Web Sites"

So this is the part where I may lose some of you as you read these words, intent on immediately saying "no way." In 25 years, with emerging media and the combination of interfaces as described above, do you really think Web sites will still be browsed as they are today using some software that reads a company's pages? We can already see the direction dictated by both consumers and marketers in halo media and the portability of content with widgets and social media.

Therefore, our future with Web sites won't look the way it has for the past 15 years. I propose that Web sites will be replaced by packets of information that are assembled for users to *experience*. Companies will provide not only their own information but the information assembled about them from the rest of the Internet. This assembly won't necessarily be in a 2D space, either. As the years go by, our browsing interfaces will change as well as computer input devices such as a mouse and keyboard. If we advance to the point of not needing these devices, imagine what our browsing experience will be like!

2002 brought us Steven Spielberg's film "Minority Report", based on the short story by Phillip K. Dick. In the movie, special effects and CGI were used to depict tool interfaces that allowed Chief John Anderton, played by Tom Cruise, to observe and engage content using his hands. Microsoft Surface™ already shows us that this can be possible using a touch-sensitive screen. The only real difference is that there was no "surface" in the movie. Visuals were all hologram-based as Cruise played out the motions in thin air on screen.

If the technology is already there, then why would we expect ourselves to point and click in the future? Companies will adapt to new user interfaces as they always have in the past. Mobile apps are already pointing the way (and the need) for marketers to develop new interfaces in order to accommodate user preferences in media.

The future interaction with companies through interactive media will be customized for the user. Each experience will be unique and allow a *virtual walk-through* and *browsing* of their goods and services. I expect there to be a lot less reading and a lot more visualization as consumers engage with brands and products in order to enhance their confidence in purchasing decisions. Although I doubt we will have holograms available by then (damnit!), I believe that everything will be presented in a much more artistic fashion, with consideration given to who we are when we visit. Browsers as they are known today will be software decipherers as packets of information from the company we are checking out will be interpreted and presented to us in an engaging format. With the cloud present, both users and publishers alike will find this possible with the storage and collective processing resources it provides.

A World *With* Advanced Advertising

Marketers in this world will be heavily reliant on community reputation, more formally today known as social media.

All public conversations in the interactive world will be monitored and intercepted in order to maintain a brand's integrity. Marketers will utilize behavioral targeting to the fullest extent and make sure they present before you even before you begin your work computing for the day.

The mashup of consumer information, conversations and behavior will be like a playground for marketers who still can't decide where to start. Our fragmentation of media and subsequent users will continue to grow and offer multiple, MULTIPLE channels for communications that will be useful in different formats for different companies.

Needless to say, consumers will still be inundated with advertising messages, so it will be imperative to develop a one-on-one relationship with them through mass media. Fortunately, technology will allow us to do this, which is a good thing since most consumers of the future will come to expect this type of interaction. The lines of privacy will become blurred as we, the marketers, will be given the opportunity to communicate with our target audience through user "preferences." Understand that as I talk about "users" in this future sense, I am referring to users of *all media*, not just computing.

Advertising formats as we know them today will be out the window when the cloud collides with and combines media engagement. New advertising will have more than 20 times the number of formats we are using today. Formats will require video, audio and animation no matter if they are Web-based or through mobile devices. Rich media will be applied to radio, television and mobile, just as it is on the Internet today. Everything will encompass interactivity. Anything that doesn't will be perceived as nothing more than a static billboard.

… And here you thought we have too many ad formats as it is today!

Chapter XV

The Speed of Information

Remember in the mid-'90s when the Web was called the "information superhighway" for a couple of years? Geez, I hated that term. I don't think anyone could have come up with a cornier name if they tried. Fortunately, we all kind of used it once or twice and then moved on to other descriptors.

But, realistically, the information superhighway is a great description of how content on the Web, mobile and other communications move and transfer. Users connect, discuss and transfer massive amounts of information on a daily basis. However, we as a human race tend to only serve as catalysts to that which is already happening virtually and automatically without hesitation.

The speed of information is what forces us to stay on top of emerging media trends and, well, "emergence" itself. It is this force that drives us and compels us to constantly be on the lookout for new technologies to apply in our professional world. Information causes everything to evolve. Not just with technology, but as a species. Newton's law says that with every action there is an equal and opposite reaction. The same goes for intangible things unseen. The more information becomes available (action), the more we adapt and modify our behavior (reaction). The sum effect of this is called *accelerated change*.

Information discovery used to take years to document, publish and manufacture into text-ridden records distributed by scholars, bookstores, professors, journals and newspapers. Even as recently as the '80s and early '90s, we were still confined to media that required the duplication of documents to make them available to the general public. While we continued going through the motions of our daily grind, we simply weren't paying attention to the digital age upon us. Information today doesn't require a printing press to be transmitted to the masses. All that's required is the transmission itself.

It's no wonder why everyone I talk to in our industry of communication seems to be overwhelmed. On a daily basis you are absorbing more information and new understandings in one day than what our civilization did in a month only within the last century or so. Go back hundreds of years, new information simply *trickled* in. No wonder Aristotle, Socrates and Plato were renowned philosophers. They *had the time* to sit around and actually use their brains for something other than deciphering information that already existed! Seriously, have you ever wondered why they are no "great philosophers" in today's world as they were known back then?

We have the first three dimensions, which are spatial and are represented by coordinates at x, y and z axes. The fourth dimension is described as time itself. There have been arguments that suggest we have up to 10 dimensions that make up physical space on the sub-atomic level alone. I propose that information occupies "space" and therefore can be found in one of those additional dimensions, in very close proximity to the fourth dimension (time). Stay tuned to discuss the correlation of information over time and how one influences the other as technology advances and progresses toward singularity.

Information itself has only been measureable since the 1940s as the term "bit" was used to measure binary digits. Transfer rates back then were very slow, with technological limitations to compute them. Today, those bits have turned into gigabytes (with 1G equal to 8,589,934,592 bits). In the 1940s, I guarantee no one knew that our information today would be measured by the following metric conversions:

1 Bit = a "1" or "0" in binary (ex. "1000" = "10101111101000" in binary representation)

*1 Byte	=	8 Bits
1 Kilobyte (KB)	=	1,000 Bytes
1 Megabyte (MB)	=	1,000 Kilobytes
1 Gigabyte (GB)	=	1,000 Megabytes
1 Terabyte (TB)	=	1,000 Gigabytes
1 Petabyte (PB)	=	1,000 Terabytes
1 Exabyte (EB)	=	1,000 Petabytes

* Rounded off to the nearest 000

To demonstrate how technology over time progresses, intersects and influences information size and speed, let's take a quick look at how the cost of information storage has changed over the years:

Year	Cost per 1 Gigabyte of Storage
1992	$1,000.00
1994	$302.50
1996	$91.51
1998	$27.68
2000	$8.37
2002	$2.53
2004	$0.77
2006	$0.23
2008	$0.07
2010	$0.02

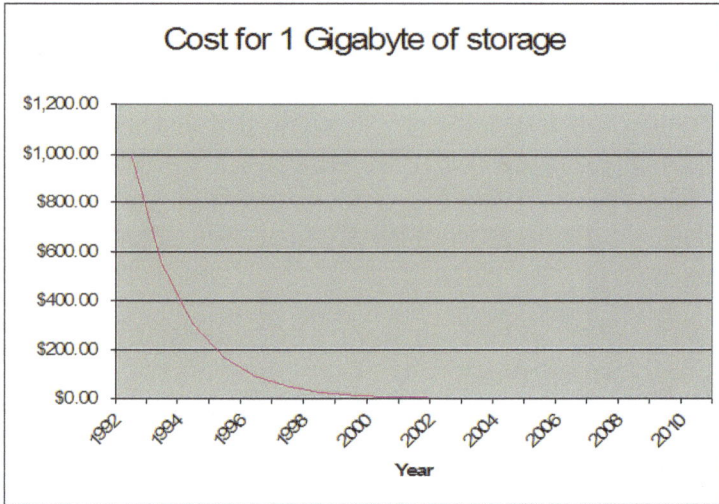

Cost for 1 Gigabyte of storage

Throughout my research, it was equally interesting to find that megabytes used to cost tens of thousands of dollars just over 50 years ago! With information available today growing at an alarming rate, storage and associated costs won't be a problem. Processing all that information is a different story.

Moore's Law

Some of you have heard of Moore's Law, some of you haven't. Truthfully, it isn't a *law of physics* such as Newton's Law of Motion. Rather it is more comparable to a *rule of thumb* based on observation, much like Murphy's Law, which states if something can go wrong, it probably will.

Moore's Law was used to define the annual trending of hardware advancement and efficiency. Gordon Moore was the co-founder of Intel when he published these observations in 1965. He related it to the number of transistors that can be added to an integrated circuit and how they increased exponentially every two years; doubling to be exact, with inexpensive (decreasing cost) associations for the consumer and manufacturer.

What I find really interesting in this law is how sustainable it is. It has held strong with regard to almost any technological advancement over the years. Looking at the advancement of components and characteristics of electronics, you will find that it relates to plasma television development, the number of pixels on digital cameras, the release of each new gaming console, each generation of cell phone microprocessor speeds and yes, memory storage capacities.

For the past 30 years, Moore's Law has been expected to last another decade. With each decade that goes by, the law remains intact. Many scientists argue that there will be a time when the law is broken and is no longer applicable to technological advancement. However, based on the past 50 years, if we were to continue down this path, we reach a theoretical and interesting destination.

Moore's Law is self-fulfilling. If we draw a line that is infinite and plot the advancements in technology (beyond the use of integrated circuits it originally referenced) to scale over time, we eventually come to a point in the future where it reaches *technological singularity* - the period of time where technology progresses *instantaneously*.

This is the part where you can reference sci-fi books and movies from your childhood. Technological singularity is believed to occur just beyond the point of the creation of artificial intelligence (AI), which stands to reason as it will probably be necessary for super intelligence to take us to this instance. When AI is first developed, there will be a series of small steps in advancement as it learns from mistakes and moves forward at an accelerated rate. If machines are able to barely advance beyond the capacity of human intelligence, they will ultimately redesign themselves in ways that couldn't be dreamed of by their own creators. Their intelligence will grow exponentially, serving as a catalyst to propel us to singularity.

So when we describe this point in time where technological advancements happen instantaneously, it doesn't seem too far-fetched to understand how we are going to interpret and decipher the correlated speed of information coming in. No one said it would be done by the *human* brain.

In addition, since memory storage has become so much cheaper than in years past, it has been noted that futuristically it will make sense to trade *space for time*. This will allow us the speed of access required to assimilate information coming in. After all, we've been able to allocate portions of our personal computer hard drive for data processing for years, why wouldn't this be done to a larger degree in the future?

Accelerated Availability

The amount of information available to us today is astounding. Google's mission statement has always been to organize the world's information and make it accessible and useful. When I first heard this upon their arrival to the search engine scene, I have to admit that I scoffed a bit at the notion of it even being a possibility to do. But with our advancements in memory capacity and processing speeds, it seems this isn't impossible at all.

In 2003 I read an article in *PC World* that stated all the information in the world doubles every three years (not too far off from Moore's exponential observations about technology itself). By 2012, information would have doubled three more times, making it eight times larger than it was in 2003.

The same article also went on to state that it would take five exabytes to hold all the world's data at the time. Today, terabyte storage has just entered the retail space. To put it in perspective: one exabyte is roughly equal to 1,000,000 terabytes.

If in 2003, five exabytes held the world's data, then by 2012, it will take 40 exabytes based on information doubling over time.

All words ever spoken by human beings take up five exabytes alone in text format.

In 2008 it was estimated that monthly Internet traffic (the total transfer of online information) consumed up to eight exabytes.

The Commonwealth Scientific and Industrial Research Organization (CSIRO) estimates that over the next decade, new telescopes will process more than one exabyte of data every four days.

There is an article I refer to and have read a number of times because it puts this accelerated availability and growth of information in perfect perspective. Being human limits us in the way we can interpret and decipher information when compared to the ultimate capabilities of a machine. While it is easier for us to absorb information rather than produce it, computers and machines can generate massive amounts of data in a very short period of time.

I encourage everyone to read the works of Kevin Kelly, founding executive editor of *Wired* magazine. Although his works are more centered on digital culture than the exclusive marketing aspects of emerging media, he has a fascinating insight into observations of the changing world around us. His article about the Speed of Information is a must-read in order to truly gain a clear perspective. Here is an excerpt from this posting (a personal favorite) written in 2006. It pertains to his assessment of the growth of information at a rate of 66 percent per year:

"It is hard to imagine anything else in the world that could possibly grow that fast. Even with information it is hard to imagine how it could continue to expand at that yearly

rate, since humans are not reproducing at that rate. How could information continue to accumulate at 66% per year for decades more? With machines. Most humans can consume more information in an hour than they generate (so much easier to watch a video than to make one) but machines can generate more information than they consume day and night. Embedded sensors, cameras with no human eyes, bots on the web, computer-run systems all generate enormous oceans of data outside of human view. It is plausible to image the global sphere of information expanding exponentially as data generation becomes mechanical.

"My conclusion: On the time scale of decades and longer, information is the fastest growing thing on this planet."

– "The Technium: *The Speed of Information*" (www.kk.org)

Transitions Posing Opportunity

Understanding the information and digital age we live in is an essential part of the innovations that marketers embark on to exploit technology as it is available today. Many marketing professionals choose to live on foundation, executing on what has been established to work for them. This group won't try new tactics until there are formal whitepapers, case studies and best practices published to hold their hands and usher them along. Other marketers enjoy taking a step back to see the big picture that exists now and just around the corner.

Once you realize how fast information moves today and how fast the capacity to accommodate the information grows, it's easier to see around the corner. Progression in development and availability makes our future world closer with every day that goes by. That's why I think *vision* is a huge commodity when it comes to marketing traits within individual professionals. Without vision, companies will always be a few steps behind.

The great thing about this vision is that our present business, technology and communication environment allows any company to take additional steps forward without much risk. In the past, we left it up to the big tech giants to introduce discoveries and new technology to be applied to tactics. But today with the massive channels of new communication being introduced, we don't necessarily need "new" technology as we are still trying different strategies with what exists.

Social media evolution is a perfect example of this. With the launch of message boards and chat rooms in the early '90s, we had these two basic channels to integrate our marketing into communities found on a few major publishers. Today, social media adds Twitter, Facebook, MySpace, WordPress, Blogger, LinkedIn, virtual worlds and more. And while we are trying to embrace as much as possible and execute in the most effective way, there is more coming on the horizon; whether we feel like we need it or not.

Even with how fast our world of data is growing, it is still a big leap between where we are now and the future as described earlier. As we move along, there are specific time periods between our present and future that are noted by introduction of new technology. These transition phases give us a huge opportunity to innovate and implement emerging media tactics that are on the verge of becoming mainstream. The more we understand about how new media works, the easier it will be to predict how our consumers will interface with it once it is acclimated.

Vision doesn't necessarily mean *action*. You can observe and make decisions on how to execute emerging media without having to spend money or resources. Part of a person's vision is research. Another portion of vision has to do with connecting the dots to speculate a future result. Taking action and stepping toward that result in the future is really the last phase of your visionary processing. A good benchmark to gauge your visionary skills is by noticing that by the time you are taking action, most of your competitors are just starting to research.

Augmented Reality (AR)

At the time of this writing, "augmented reality" is making headlines again as new discoveries in programming are being made. There are still a lot of unknowns as to where this will take us in the future of marketing which is why I chose not to make it a chapter by itself. Yet, it's an excellent example of a *transition phase* toward the future of media that marketers with vision will soon be taking advantage of.

Augmented reality is the end result of computerized data or graphics and imagery overlaid onto real video footage in real time. For those of you who make a connection through a simple practical example, think of the yellow "first down" markers in football games on television. The term was first coined in the 1990s and has been an area of scientific research for quite some time. But with recent advancements and applications, it is at the point where marketers with vision should start taking notice.

In February 2002 *Popular Science* magazine published an article about AR without much attention from the advertising industry. Back then, the first MARS (mobile augmented reality system) had been developed by Columbia University as the journalist conveyed his own experience testing the prototype. The system was bulky, requiring a 26-pound backpack and headgear, accompanied by an oversized shoulder-mounted antenna and batteries that were described to be the size of soap bars. Walking around with this equipment enabled the user to see text callouts (generated by GPS) that were overlaid onto the images seen through the special glasses worn as they walk down the street. Obviously, it wasn't something to be worn by the general public anytime soon. This application is now referred to as *mobile augmented reality*.

AR existed well before then with even my own recollections as a kid being at the Haunted Mansion inside Disneyland and noticing a skeleton riding in my car when I looked at the mirror.

More recently, GE started using AR as a way to communicate their Smart Grid. Shortly after, I viewed hundreds of videos created and posted of people interacting with GE's expressive way of presenting a boring topic. Using a personal Web cam and a piece of paper with a solid image for the camera to detect, users were able to hold the paper up to the camera and watch the screen as a digital hologram emerged from their own hands.

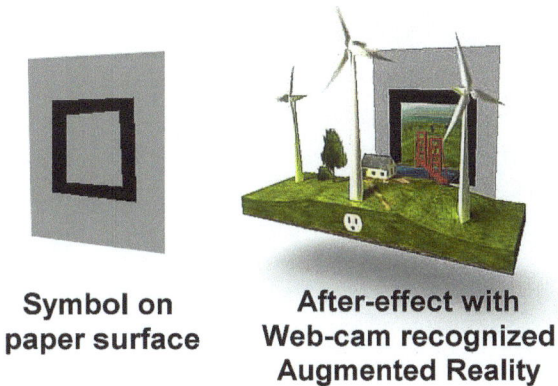

Symbol on paper surface

After-effect with Web-cam recognized Augmented Reality

Now AR has the attention it needs to start becoming a more common marketing tactic within the next year or two. To the consumer it is an amusement. To the marketer, it's a step toward another viable emerging media channel.

You can clearly see how you need two things to make emerging media happen - the technology itself and consumer adaptation. In this case, as in most examples, the technology has been around for over a decade. However, the consumer adaptation has taken this long to finally justify a campaign with reach using this media. Web cams have now become so inexpensive and compact that manufacturers are now building them into the monitor. This enables our audience to effectively experience AR.

Just as the Web cams enabled users to observe and interact with AR, cell phones and PDA devices will soon allow users to appreciate mobile AR. The article in *Popular Science* was written before Moore's Law took effect on GPS and PDA processors. Seven years later, with the advancement in size and efficiency multiplied more than five times, mobile AR is *just around the corner*.

AR has reached a point where marketers can certainly see the next steps that will be available to them. Promotional messaging services that interpolate text ads with visuals seen through mobile AR glasses (or cell phone digital camera viewfinders) will soon be offered to us as easily as text ads in search marketing. The only thing to do is sit back and wait for the opportunity to jump.

Chapter XVI
Final Thoughts and
Rules of Thumb

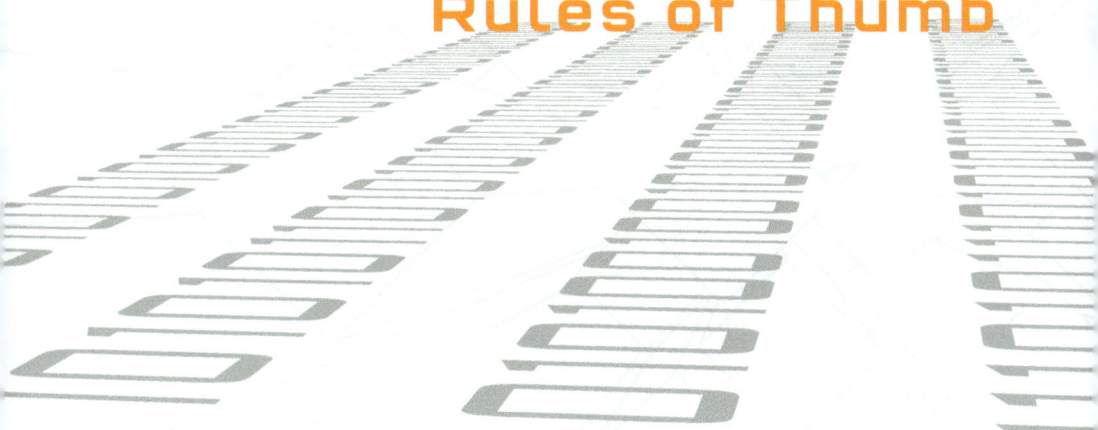

Future media in theory and actual media available to us today in marketing change rapidly. What was once thought to be years away from us is happening right now. The vision of things to come will be here tomorrow. This book highlighted both areas and has equipped you with tools to execute what you can do right now while attempting to explain the mindset needed to develop your arsenal in the future.

There are a few thoughts and ideas I wanted to express in this book but felt could be saved for this section. These overall points are things that I've kept in mind over the years while working alongside people like you with similar interests in emerging media.

Don't Lose Focus

With time comes new understanding based on new information. It is very possible that much of what we assume about the future may take a dramatic change with the introduction of new technology. Emerging media and marketing theories for strategy will also change accordingly. The important thing to remember is not to "fall in love" with a concept of the future. It's interesting and entertaining many times to think about the new possibilities in media exploration and communication, but your primary objective should be to build and service your company today. Anything hedged on future technologies or an unexplored medium should take a back seat when it comes to profitability right now.

Measurement Is Critical

As mentioned earlier in this book, measurement IS and ALWAYS WILL BE critical. None of us work for companies that don't care where their money is spent. Practicality in metric usage and appropriate benchmark establishment is necessary to make your work with emerging media notable and professional. It is vitally important to your future success that you measure each step, document every result, and quantify any returns. This will make your triumphs well-rounded with description and trump other marketing comments that come your way saying, "You *should* try this ...." You will be able to easily answer with, "Been there, done that, here are the results," without spending additional time proving or disproving someone else's incorrect perception of what works.

Wear Your Customer's Shoes

When considering new technology in advertising, be sure to fully understand the media and its usage by the public. Take a walk around and make observations in different social circles to see who's using what and how they are using it. Constantly remind yourself to put yourself in your customer's shoes. How would you like to be messaged to? What kind of message would get you to purchase or become a fan of a brand?

Often times it is easier to lose sight of the customer experience because we are too close to the campaign. It's always been a good practice to take a look around you and try to meet the *realistic needs* and *practical desires* of interactive users.

Low-Hanging Fruit First

We would all love to dive right into all the cool, new media surrounding us and be the next company on the cover of *Ad Age*. As glamorous as it may sound, I believe that good marketers utilizing emerging media have already ensured their employers have addressed the basics. By *basics* I'm referring to the *basics of interactive marketing*. Since *interactive* characteristics of marketing are largely found within Web marketing application, this would mean Internet marketing in general.

Whenever any of my contacts are hired as marketing directors or vice presidents, they are always excited and ready to jump in to prove themselves. As you make your way through the ranks of coordinator and management, you are already proving yourself in terms of work ethic and capability. Engaging "new media" isn't by any means a measurement of your marketing capability. If there are tried and true Internet marketing tactics that your company isn't doing, there's no reason to chase after unproven emerging media channels that have no established rules or best practices.

Emerging media strategy should come *after* the basics are covered. Without a foundation of Internet/interactive advertising such as search marketing, behavioral targeting, CPC campaigns, proper Web analytics, etc., you will have no ROI collectively to justify mistakes. And mistakes *are very common* in emerging media executions. If you spent twice as much on a failed new media strategy compared against what you spent and made in total revenue across all channels, chances are that your execution of the basics will cover your error. But if the foundation of basics hasn't been established, you have no cover and will be naked in the middle of the street with everyone noticing.

One of the companies I've worked for spent more time trying to adopt emerging media than they did on covering their basic interactive channels. I don't know if this is driven by ego, senior management expectations or just pure pursuit of the "cool factor." But it is amazing the hours, money and resources that are wasted in this quest without the foundational support of other programs that have already been proven. How are you going to measure the success of your social media efforts without proper Web analytics? Why spend a lot of money on mobile marketing if your current email marketing is fragmented at best? Does a viral campaign or widget development really make sense without a Web site that's been optimized for online sales?

The competitive nature of interactive marketers can drive us to overlook what we should already be doing. We all want to be on top of our game. But, realistically, you are doing a great disservice to your company, client or employer by ignoring the things that are already out there and proven to be strong ROI generators. There's always time to go after the *new*, just be sure that you've already gone after the *old*, because I will tell you today - it still works. It's much easier to show returns on what has already been navigated than it is to show returns in uncharted territory.

Forget the "Rules"

... because there are *none*. Experienced marketing professionals entering an emerging media space will need to pull everything they can *from their own experience* and *their own research*. One of the biggest characteristics of emerging media is that there are no rules to follow, few case studies to read, and barely any best practices available for reference.

This is an area that hasn't been engaged enough to create industry standards, which is why it is important to draw conclusions based on your own observations and past *experience*. You can minimize the egg on your face if you plot your course based on what you know from the past. A knowledge base of your consumers, similar campaigns from the past, and thorough understanding of how emerging media works from your perspective as a user will serve you well and give you a small torch to light the way.

This is the best scenario of tools available to assist with navigation. Since you don't necessarily want to discuss the potential returns with your own competitors, talk about it with marketers in other companies you have noticed using the same tactic as part of their own marketing mix. I suggest calling them directly. It's easy to delete email and ignore a stranger's request for guidance. A personal call to the marketing manager, director or vice president of a company using emerging media will get you a much better response. Every time I've called marketing professionals from an industry other than my own to discuss their emerging media endeavors, I've always been met with a positive response. More often than not, they are excited to hear that other *marketers* are taking notice of their new ventures, and you can quickly ascertain the passion in their voice. Although your industries are completely different, they will be very forthcoming about the underlying principles that have made the new media a success (or failure) for them, from which you can draw a loose execution blueprint of your own.

You are THE Trendsetter and Opinion Leader

In social media we are always looking for big brand advocates, fans and most importantly those with influential capabilities within their networks of contacts. While there are trendsetters within consumer groups that adopt new media and influence purchase decisions, we serve as opinion leaders as well. We are the ones who qualify different media as an advertising, marketing or promotional communications tool. Our testing and trialing of new methods through emerging media is observed by other marketing professionals standing on the sidelines.

In order for emerging media to take off and be utilized by the masses in business marketing it has to be proven to generate beneficial ROI. As we pioneer new strategies through the next generation of advertising channels, we are indirectly carving a path for other marketing professionals to follow. Be thrilled to know that when you are taking steps toward the unknown, you are literally assembling an advertising model that may be the benefactor of billions in future marketing budgets.

Three conscious actions *during* your emerging media ventures will identify you as having a strong professional mindset in your practice:

> **Question** – no matter what you've "heard." Always pose questions and challenges to new media. Just because it has worked for someone else doesn't mean it will work for you. Your industry may be unique, your budget may be too small, and your audience may be completely different. Always proceed with caution and be upfront with your questions. At the same time, be prepared for no concrete answers. This is new territory for you and others. Identifying the fact that there isn't an answer to a question can be just as insightful as getting an answer itself.

> **Test** – and test again. Compose all the different scenarios possible and push them out there for evaluation. Is there only one type of placement? Is this the correct messaging? Should I target other audiences within this channel? These are just a few

of the questions that should lead to different tests. Test as long as you can afford it or until you are satisfied that you have disqualified or qualified the medium as being a potential business driver.

Defy – especially when someone claims they struck gold and *"everyone should be doing it."* When entering an area within emerging media, I always look to be as critical and as nay-saying as I possibly can when it seems things are "hyped." Never be afraid to talk smack about something you tried that doesn't work for you. If you've done your homework, tested thoroughly and asked the right questions in the process, you should be just as vocal about something not working as you would be if you discovered the Holy Grail itself. This will save the advertising world a lot of time if something is hyped to be something it's not. Some people keep their failures to themselves. I guess the utilitarianism in me tends to think we should all learn from one another's mistakes and that life is too short to allow others to make the same mistakes as we all search for the next big thing in media.

Final Thoughts on the Future

The next 25 years are going to be *awesome,* after which they will be *unrecognizable.* That is, unrecognizable to you and me. Right now, in my mid-thirties, I have the opportunity to associate with both the older, seasoned generation as well as the younger marketers just a few years out of college. Let me say that watching and listening to these two groups converse can gain you more insight than you know what to do with. The older professionals have seen the migration from offline to online as well as media merging together. The younger group has grown up using emerging media as part of their own lifestyle. Combining old-school marketing principles with fresh-minded know-how is like an explosion of creative energy.

Although the older professionals I'm speaking of are quite progressive in applying new media into their marketing strategies, unfortunately from my observations the rest of this demographic is slow to do the same. I mentioned earlier that the baby-boomer, blue-hair generation still sitting on the board of directors, overextending their employment before retirement is responsible for the pace of emerging media progression. People fear what they don't understand and at some point get to an age where they feel their understanding of new applications and tactics is not necessary for survival.

If there's a new media I don't understand, you can bet that I'm researching, discussing and writing down everything I can until there's comprehension. If that means using it for daily communications and as part of my lifestyle, so be it. I am still in the part of a career where you have to stay competitive in order to be a desired commodity in today's business.

But the baby-boomer generation entering retirement age looks at it differently. If it makes money, do it. If it doesn't, don't do it. Either way, just don't expect them to embrace the new initiative using new media as passionately as you do. Their sense of "why-take-a-chance?" thinking has already overridden the entrepreneurial spirit they may have had back in their day. Unfortunately, this attitude is present on the boards of the largest brand-name companies today with the largest budgets for advertising. Emerging media may find a few marketers to take advantage of it, but until the baby boomers leave their offices for retirement village, the current pace of breakthrough will stay.

Their generation has started to retire. Economical conditions might mean they have to stick around a little while, but I'd say they'll only be around for another five or six years from now. Shortly thereafter, there will be a burst of new media tactics reaching us faster than ever before. So when I say "the next 25 years will be awesome," this would be one of the reasons. When I say "after which it will be unrecognizable," it has more to do with you and I.

While you were still living with your parents, you probably remember them asking you to set up the digital clocks whenever the power went out. I grew up in the Midwest, so every time we had a thunderstorm it was guaranteed to be a chore for me by the time I got home. The clocks, the VCR, the answering machine and I were all good friends. My folks were more than happy to stay out of that relationship, because *learning technology* as it came out back then took more time than they felt like spending. Whereas I had grown up with these components and thoroughly understood how they worked.

I could never understand why my parents would blow off the coolness of technology and how it can help you manage your life. I can happily say today that they can set their own digital clocks and have actually turned into avid computer users. It was only recently that I came to the understanding of why they were the way they were back then.

As everyone approaches the middle-aged phase of his or her life, it is going to be tougher to stay on top of the media trends of consumer usage for the majority of us. Family, bills, houses, cars, jobs and everything that fills up our "off" time grows to the point where it squeezes out the time we used to use for "free thinking." A 23-year-old college graduate has more time than he knows what to do with. He gets older, gets married, has kids, buys a house or two, and slowly fills his time that used to be free. It's much more difficult to spend time learning new technologies than it is to ask or pay someone else to do it. Of course I don't regret having kids and growing a family, it just means that I have to *consciously* make time for emerging media research, much like everyone else looking to stay competitive in his or her field.

Gradually, the release of new media will pass us by and will only be truly understood and utilized by today's youth. The speed and volume of information they will have the capability to assimilate will be absolutely dumbfounding. They too, will be in a world with more than eight times the information available today. So, yes, after 25 years or so of emerging media introduction to the marketplace, it will be unrecognizable to you and me through no other fault than the natural life cycles of the human race.

Emerging media and the speed of information transfer have made us more proactive and attentive toward the next generation of advertising. Although I think it will definitely pass up our own understanding at some point in the distant future, I don't think we'll have the same situation as we do now with baby boomers stunting its progress. The new human race will be more productive than ever with the acceleration in tools technology continues to give us. Marketing, advertising and media will never grow stale. We will be presented with infinite opportunities during transitions in technology. Always question, test and defy. And while you are at it - discover, evaluate and *evolve*.

eMarketer™
DIGITAL INTELLIGENCE

As you've read this book you probably noticed a number of references to eMarketer research. I thought it appropriate to highlight this invaluable service that has assisted me as an employee and contractor for well-known brands in web publishing, hospitality, legal and entertainment industries.

Since 2000 I've used eMarketer research as a primary source of statistics, competitive studies and media trends for decisions in budgeting, online strategy and new media investments. The research is presented in an easy to understand format that is essential for marketers today using it on-the-fly or for extensive planning and market analysis.

There are many other research companies I've used for both digital and offline advertising, but I have yet to find one that presents data from all channels in a comprehensive manner the way eMarketer does. Their in-depth forecasts are a road map for conclusive opportunities. The fact that they compile their information from thousands of different sources also ensures each report, graph or article employs cross-referenced summaries with freshly mined data.

I cannot recommend their services enough and highly suggest adding them to your arsenal as our digital media world continues to accelerate. www.emarketer.com

-S

Other Recommendations

I'm often asked for recommendations based on services I've had direct experience with when it comes to new media channels. As you look to outsource some of your projects, you will find that many service providers and agencies out there are fairly young, often times in their start-up phase.

While I feel it's encouraging to know there are new media companies available to service our needs as marketers, there are a few in particular I have found to be leaders in different categories. As media service providers grow, they mature in their experiences with clients, technology development and data pulled from their own case studies. When venturing into new media, it's important to ensure those working on your teams are well-versed in navigating the waters.

The level of professionalism and client support I've received from these entities is second-to-none. I advise everyone I speak with to consider them while seeking more information about mobile marketing, video distribution, in-game advertising and social media campaigns.

I always keep an eye out for new companies to test-drive emerging media applications. Considering everyone's knowledge in a particular area is vital to continue our understanding of progression and channel availability. These are a few I've come across that are tried and true.

Cellit

Cellit Marketing is truly the best mobile marketing service provider I have found in today's mobile marketing industry. Their approach toward new clients entering the mobile marketing realm accommodates both seasoned and first-time companies looking to take advantage of this media channel.

Cellit introduces mobile marketing through an educational approach that surpasses any other company I've experienced in this area. Their dedication to ensuring client knowledge base and comfort reaches above and beyond what anyone would normally expect from service providers.

Since its formation, Cellit has received considerable attention for their self-service, web-based model for mobile marketing solutions. They walk all their clients (both large and small) through a step-by-step process, making it quickly adaptable and accepted into routine operation.

They are a member of the Mobile Marketing Association and work with a number of large-brand name companies in assisting their mobile marketing needs. I've evaluated a number of different companies in this space and feel Cellit is the best in terms of price, service and ultimate desire to educate their clients on mobile marketing applications.

www.cellitmarketing.com

dei worldwide

In "Chapter 4 – Social Media", it goes without saying that I would highly recommend the services of DEI Worldwide. They have been a resource for many Fortune 500 companies today with good reason. Their ethical approach to conversational marketing online has set the bar for other agencies to follow.

Consistent enforcement of proper "rules of engagement" is found within their company as their CEO, David Reis, is also a co-founder of WOMMA and strong supporter of practical blog campaign applications.

My personal experience with them suggests nothing other than a top-notch, professional social media services firm. Their post-campaign reporting is as robust as any emerging marketer could ask for as they are completely transparent in their tactics, executions and strategy.

If you are looking for a social media solutions agency to accommodate your current efforts or assist in newly developed campaigns, DEI Worldwide should be a starting point as you evaluate current solutions available.

www.deiworldwide.com

DBG

Digital Broadcasting Group

Digital Broadcast Group (DBG) is one of the premier video production and distribution services on the Web today. I've had the opportunity to work with them extensively in the past and have always been impressed with their level of professionalism and knowledge base. While formulating your video production and execution, DBG takes a hands-on approach to assimilating your defined goals and objective into a well-thought execution strategy.

Emerging Marketer discussed video as a means to reach the masses using multiple platforms for engagement. DBG is well-versed in all areas and has been the best solution I've found to accommodate my campaigns and messaging. They offer a complete start-to-finish solution from development to distribution within their network hosting over 100 million users to reach your audience goals.

Their in-house production department has never disappointed me as it has always been a collaborative experience to work through. After production and development, it was a seamless next-step with distributions. DBG is a great resource to consider when working toward video execution through any interactive channels.

www.dbgroup.tv

massive

Massive Incorporated is the largest in-game advertising network available to interactive marketers today. My experience with them stems from years of client-side relationship advertising where they played a strong role in facilitating in-game executions. Their measurement for in-game impression-based advertising is second-to-none within this emerging media sector.

Massive provides placement across all pre-defined Xbox 360 game titles, allowing the client to target based on time of day, demographic, and content. Microsoft has helped shaped this company to be one of the leaders in this media category which they demonstrate through client education, campaign optimization and reporting.

Gaming is one of the fastest growing global forms of entertainment and presents unique marketing opportunities for brands targeting hard-to-reach consumers. With the gaming audience described as a desired demographic in this book, Massive presents a viable opportunity to reach them.

www.massiveincorporated.com

About the Author

Shawn Rorick is a digital media professional with over 15 years experience in web development, Internet marketing and next-generation advertising. Witnessing the boom of Las Vegas and working as Marketing Director for large corporations such as Cox Communications, MGM MIRAGE and Cirque du Soleil, he has gained the insight and experience to accurately describe our new media today while providing a road-map description of our future. Shawn has been requested to speak at a number of marketing conferences, recently serving as opening keynote and track publisher for PubCon. He has been quoted by executives as being responsible for "single-handedly dragging Las Vegas advertising into the 21st century".

With hands-on experience in web development, interactive media planning and direct marketing execution, Shawn has trained, coached and educated many "emerging marketers" today. His expertise has been sought after by companies in a variety of industries utilizing interactive media to reach their valued customers. Shawn is a graduate of Southern Illinois University with a double bachelor's in Business Management and Marketing with Applied Science Degrees in Technology. In recent years, he founded and chaired the Las Vegas Interactive Marketing Association, with over 500 members today.

Shawn is also the author of EmergingMarketer.com assisting several business units operating within the digital space including gaming, affiliate, social media, and Bluetooth. He currently resides in Las Vegas dedicating his career to educating marketers from all disciplines and backgrounds seeking to apply successful emerging media channels to their marketing endeavors.